SHADOW WORK
Journal & Workbook

An in-depth Guide based on Carl Jung's Work

Free Shadow Work Meditation

Embark on a meditation journey that goes beyond mere contemplation—it's a deep, interactive exchange with your shadow self. Delve into its depths, guided at each turn, to not just witness but actively converse with your innermost layers. This isn't your everyday meditation; it's an enlightening chat with the unsung parts of you.

Ready to start this introspective dialogue? Dive in at felixbuchwald.com/meditation or simply scan the QR code below.

Get to know your Shadow

SHADOW WORK MEDITATION

ACCESS FOR FREE AT
FELIXBUCHWALD.COM/MEDITATION

Commitment to My Future Self

Take a moment to sit comfortably. Close your eyes and, in alignment with your highest self, imagine the best version of yourself a year from now. What are you doing? How do you feel? What changes have you made? Breathing deeply, see the strength you've nurtured, the inner peace you've cultivated, and the warmth you radiate.

I, _____, hereby pledge to passionately journey towards my envisioned self. With each word I pen in this journal, I am firmly shaping my path ahead. With an open heart, I commit to each entry, embracing the process with a readiness to learn. As I step into the mirror of self-reflection, I look forward to the personal growth that lies ahead, knowing every thought penned is a step towards that envisioned future. With this intentional commitment, I lay the foundation for my transformation.

_____

SIGNATURE

_____

DATE

CONTENTS

Introduction

SHADOW WORK IN A NUTSHELL

Know Thyself

"To confront a person with his shadow is to show him his own light." - Carl G. Jung

The ancient Greeks had a saying: "Know thyself." Easy enough, right? Yet, here we stand, millennia later, still wrestling with those two words. Who are we? What hides in the recesses of our minds? What is it about the human psyche that, even after so many generations, remains the final frontier?

Imagine standing on the edge of an expansive and unknown forest. This forest represents your mind — vast, untamed, and filled with both awe-inspiring beauty and shadows. Shadows that hold parts of you that have long been forgotten, overlooked, or perhaps intentionally buried. This book is your compass and guide to traversing that forest, to embracing and understanding those shadows, and to emerging as a more whole, self-aware individual.

Hi there! I'm Felix, your guide for this ride. Over the last 15 years, I've been backpacking through this mental wilderness. With Shadow Work as my Swiss Army knife, I've navigated the rollercoaster of emotions, revelations, and those 'Aha!' moments.

But why should you care about my journey? Because the path I've traveled, the insights I've gleaned, the challenges I've faced, are not unique to just me. They are universally human. Whether you're just beginning your quest for self-understanding or have been on this path for years, this book provides valuable insights and tools tailored for every step of your journey.

Now, flipping through these pages is like rummaging through a treasure box in an old attic (minus the dust!). After this introduction, Part I takes us on a deep-sea exploration into the fascinating world of Shadow Work. Ever had one of those moments where you've stopped, a tad baffled, thinking, "Why did I just snap like that?" or "Where's that emotion even coming from?"— get ready to delve deeper into those enigmas. Think of these pages as a treasure map where 'X' doesn't mark danger but the keys to understanding those fascinating quirks, behaviors, and feelings that make you, well, uniquely you. And then Part II hits you with a swirl of interactive journaling prompts. And here's the fun bit—you can dive into these anytime. Midnight musings? Weekend reflections? Go wild! They're designed to weave into your journey whenever you please.

What is the Shadow?

"Until you make the unconscious conscious, it will direct your life and you will call it fate."
– Carl G. Jung

Ah, the elusive Shadow! It sounds mysterious, doesn't it? Like something out of a gripping thriller or a dark fantasy novel. But while it might conjure up images of doppelgängers and ghostly figures, in the world of psychology, the "Shadow" has an entirely different, albeit equally fascinating, connotation.

Let's start with a stroll down memory lane. Picture yourself as a kid – vibrant, free, with not a care in the world. One day, you're belting out your favorite song (off-key, mind you) in the middle of the grocery store. Suddenly, a stern look from a parent or a giggle from a passerby makes you realize that maybe your impromptu concert wasn't as appreciated as you thought. You tuck away that boisterous, carefree part of yourself, thinking, "Maybe it's best if I sing in private."

That "tucking away" process? That's the beginning of forming the Shadow. Now, you might wonder, why "Shadow"? In the simplest terms, the Shadow represents that aspect of us we can't see, much like how in a dim room, certain corners remain hidden from our eyes. We call the subconscious a "shadow" primarily because we remain unaware of it, just like how we remain oblivious to objects lurking in the darkness. On the contrary, we dub the conscious as the "light", because, well, it's right there— visible and known. Now, hold onto your hats: the majority of our mental iceberg—about 90% of it—lies submerged in the unconscious waters, with a modest 10% peeking above the conscious surface.

In the realm of Jungian psychology, the Shadow isn't some spooky, supernatural entity. Instead, it's the repository for parts of ourselves that we've swept to the sidelines, frequently because of societal norms, personal traumas, or instilled beliefs. These are aspects we might regard as undesirable or inappropriate. Over time, as these repressed facets accumulate, they can manifest in myriad ways: the fibs we weave, the power struggles we're embroiled in, our moments of self-doubt, tendencies towards neuroticism, trust issues we can't dispel, emotional roller-coasters, being controlling, cynicism, outbursts of anger, or even behaviors that appear cowardly or overly sexualized.

However, it's a widespread misconception to believe that the Shadow houses only the negatives. Yes, a substantial portion of the human shadow comprises what many consider "undesirable" primarily because we deny, disown, or push away those parts of us we label negative. But it's essential to remember that the Shadow also cradles suppressed potentials, talents, and passions. The artistic flair stifled by a discouraging remark or the leadership knack dulled by rejection fears—both find a spot in the Shadow.

Engaging with the Shadow is not about battling an opponent; it's about illumination and integration. It's about casting a light on these obscured facets, understanding them, and embracing them back into our conscious self.

How to do Shadow Work

"The gold is in the dark." - Carl G. Jung

Alright, adventurers, before we set off on this exciting trek into the wild forests of our psyche, let's get something straight: this is just the appetizer. A taste. A teaser. We'll dig deeper, climb higher, and perhaps even spelunk (that's a fun word, right?) into the cavernous regions of these techniques in the chapters to come. But for now, let's get our feet wet and understand the basics of Shadow Work.

Setting the Intention

Before we get our hands dirty, we need to set a clear intention. Why? Well, imagine you're sailing without a compass. Not so fun, right? Setting an intention is like having that compass – it guides our exploration and provides clarity. Whisper to yourself, "I am ready to face my Shadow with love and acceptance."

Embrace Curiosity

Remember being a child and asking "why" about everything? Why is the sky blue? Why do dogs bark? Channel that inner child again. As you dive deeper into your psyche, let that incessant "why" guide you. Be the detective of your own mind.

Meditation & Mindfulness

Shadow work isn't just about thinking; it's about feeling. Meditation is our gateway. By calming the mind and focusing on our breath, we create a safe space to confront the suppressed emotions and experiences lurking within. Picture it as your internal safe haven, where you can invite your Shadow to tea and have a candid chat.

Journaling: The Soul's Diary

Your Shadow has stories to tell, and what better way to capture them than in a journal? And hey, no need for Shakespearean prose. Jot down whatever surfaces, even if it's as chaotic as a toddler's art project.

Dialogue with the Shadow

Now, this might sound a smidge eccentric, but bear with me. Imagine having a conversation with your Shadow. Yep, you heard me! Ask it questions. "Why are you here?" "What do you want me to understand?" Listen to its answers. Often, this dialogue can unearth profound insights that our conscious mind overlooks.

Seek Guidance

While the allure of solitary journeys is undeniable, sometimes a guiding hand can make all the difference. Whether it's professional counsel or a supportive community, external perspectives can shine a light where we might see only darkness.

Celebrate the Unearthing

Shadow work is no walk in the park. So, when you unearth a hidden aspect of yourself and navigate through its layers, take a moment to bask in your accomplishment. Whether it's treating yourself to something special or merely acknowledging your progress, every bit of recognition counts.

And there you have it, a bite-sized guide to Shadow Work. As we delve deeper in the following chapters, you'll be equipped with the tools, the know-how, and the confidence to navigate this fascinating journey.

The Benefits of Shadow Work

"One does not become enlightened by imagining figures of light, but by making the darkness conscious." - Carl G. Jung

So, you've been reading about Shadow Work, and it's probably got you thinking, "Why on Earth would I want to poke around in those dark corners?" Well, my dear friend, that's like asking why someone would want to dig for treasure. Because that's what Shadow Work is – a treasure hunt of the soul. Allow me to enlighten you on what awaits you when you bravely embrace this transformative journey.

Healing Past Traumas

Imagine having a splinter in your foot. It's tiny, but oh, does it sting with every step! Past traumas are like those splinters, affecting every stride in life. Shadow Work is your pair of trusty tweezers, gently drawing out these painful fragments and allowing the healing to begin.

Fostering Authentic Relationships

When you understand your triggers and suppressed emotions, your interactions with others transform. You no longer project your unresolved issues onto them. The result? Foster connections with others that feel as warm and fuzzy as a cup of hot cocoa on a cold day.

Increased Creativity and Innovation

Think of your mind as a garden. The Shadow? It's like the weeds. But oh, what beautiful weeds they can be if you know how to tend to them! By embracing and integrating those shadowy aspects, you unblock channels of creativity.

Living Authentically

Ever feel like you're playing a role, putting on masks to fit in? Shadow Work strips away those masks, allowing you to embrace your true, authentic self. It's like getting to dance in the rain without worrying about who's watching.

Deepened Spiritual Connection

By embracing every part of you, the good, the bad, and the shadowy, you develop a profound connection with the universe, the divine, or whatever higher power resonates with you. It's like tuning your soul's radio to the clearest, most harmonious station.

Living with Purpose and Authenticity

No more facades. No more pretending. With Shadow Work, you shed the layers that aren't truly 'you'. In their place, you embrace your genuine self, allowing you to live with passion, clarity, and an unwavering sense of purpose.

Increased Emotional Resilience

Think of this as emotional weightlifting. By facing and integrating the repressed aspects of yourself, you become emotionally stronger. Life's curveballs? You catch them and throw them right back, with a smile!

Understanding Thyself

Ever fancied being the Sherlock Holmes of your own psyche? We all crave that deep self-awareness, don't we?

By diving into our internal mysteries and peeling back the layers, we're on a personal detective quest. Each revelation, every found clue, nudges us closer to understanding our true essence.

Becoming Whole

Every time you integrate a part of your Shadow, you're not just removing barriers or healing wounds, you're moving towards wholeness. You're bridging the gaps that once made you feel fragmented. The more you embrace and understand, the closer you get to being your true, authentic self.

Now, I get it. This might sound like a dazzling infomercial promising the sun, the moon, and the stars. But trust in the process, and you'll find that these benefits aren't just lofty promises. From my own experience, I can tell you they're genuine, attainable outcomes. Your Shadow might seem like a daunting companion at first, but as you work together, you'll realize it's one of the most valuable allies you could ever wish for. Moving towards wholeness is a journey, but it's a journey worth every step.

Behind the Shadow: Carl Jung's Foundational Work

"Your visions will become clear only when you can look into your own heart. Who looks outside, dreams; who looks inside, awakes."
- Carl G. Jung

Picture this: Vienna in the early 20th century. Pioneering psychologists, Sigmund Freud and Carl Jung, are delving deep into the human psyche. Freud, ever the methodical thinker, perceives our subconscious as a cauldron of suppressed desires (yes, many of them tantalizingly controversial). Meanwhile, Jung, once closely associated with Freud, charts a different course. He introduces us to the 'Collective Unconscious', a realm brimming with stories, memories, and symbols shared by all of humanity.

Within this realm, the Shadow is crucial. It isn't just a personal reservoir of our suppressed selves, but also a collection of societal taboos, inherited fears, and shared traumas. By confronting our Shadow, we're not only addressing our personal disowned parts but also connecting with collective elements that have been pushed away or misunderstood across generations.

Jung's dedication to understanding the unconscious led him on a personal journey of introspection, prominently documented in his journal, the 'Red Book'. Through a technique he termed 'active imagination', he engaged in dialogues with aspects from his unconscious, each representing various facets of his psyche.

For over 16 years, Jung meticulously documented these inner encounters. But the 'Red Book' was not just any journal; it was a vibrant fusion of his conscious reflections and unconscious manifestations. Filled with ornate calligraphy, detailed illustrations, and evocative paintings, all crafted by Jung himself, it became a tangible record of his inner world.

Fast-forwarding to today, the Shadow still casts its... well, shadow. Modern-day tools like Cognitive-Behavioral Therapy (CBT) help us unearth and reshape hidden biases. EMDR, designed for trauma survivors, helps shine a light on buried parts of the psyche. And Depth Therapy? That's a deep dive into our shadowy corners, revealing stories we never knew we held.

From vintage Vienna to our digital age, the quest to understand our inner self is a tale as old as time, and dear reader, it's one that we're all part of. Welcome aboard!

Pause for a moment, closing your eyes and taking several deep, calming breaths. Allow your mind to wander, honing in on persistent emotions that often simmer just below your conscious awareness. It might be an undercurrent of sadness, a sudden spark of anger, or a nebulous feeling of restlessness.

Identifying the Emotion: *Write down the emotion you feel. If you're struggling to name it, describe the sensations or images it brings to mind. Take your time with this and be detailed.*

Source of the Emotion: *Try to trace back when you first started feeling this way. Was there a specific event or series of events that might have ignited or intensified this emotion? Jot down any memories or triggers that come to mind.*

Exploring the Layers: *Often, our emotions are like onions with many layers. Beneath anger, there might be hurt; beneath sadness, there might be a feeling of abandonment. Dive deeper: What lies beneath the primary emotion you've identified?*

Visualizing the Shadow: *Close your eyes and imagine your Shadow. What does it look like? Is it a figure, a shape, or perhaps something more abstract? Capture your Shadow's appearance through words, or if you prefer, sketch a picture.*

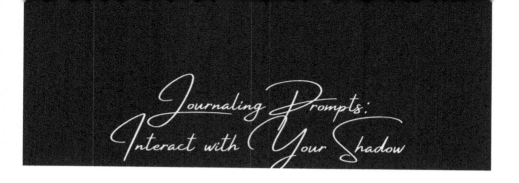

Journaling Prompts:
Interact with Your Shadow

Understanding the Shadow's Role: *The Shadow is not your enemy; it's an aspect of yourself. Write down what role you think your Shadow plays in your life. Does it protect you? Challenge you? Both?*

Inviting a Conversation: *Imagine inviting your Shadow to sit with you for a conversation. You can set the scene in your favorite quiet spot, like a cozy living room or a peaceful garden. What would you ask your Shadow? What might it say in response?*

Feeling the Connection: *How does it feel to engage with your Shadow this way? Do you feel fear, curiosity, empathy? Recognize and embrace these feelings as natural responses to getting to know a hidden part of yourself.*

Embracing the Mystery: *Your Shadow is complex and might not reveal everything at once. Write a commitment to yourself to continue exploring and inviting your Shadow into your conscious awareness.*

End this exercise with an affirmation of acceptance for your Shadow, recognizing it as a part of you that has wisdom and insight to offer. The more you engage, the more harmonious your relationship with your Shadow will become.

I am who I am and that is enough

PART I

Exploring the Depths of Shadow Work

CHAPTER ONE

Mapping the Wounds of the Soul: From Hurt to Healing

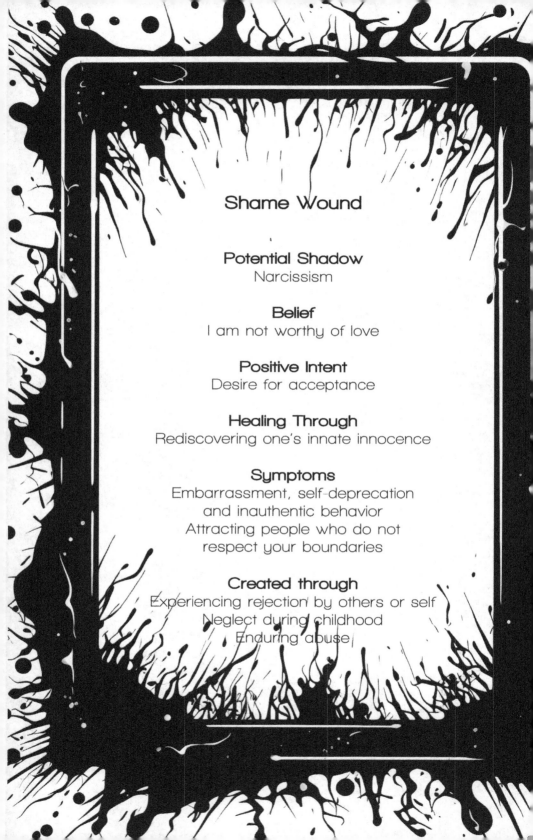

Shame Wound

Potential Shadow
Narcissism

Belief
I am not worthy of love

Positive Intent
Desire for acceptance

Healing Through
Rediscovering one's innate innocence

Symptoms
Embarrassment, self-deprecation
and inauthentic behavior
Attracting people who do not
respect your boundaries

Created through
Experiencing rejection by others or self
Neglect during childhood
Enduring abuse

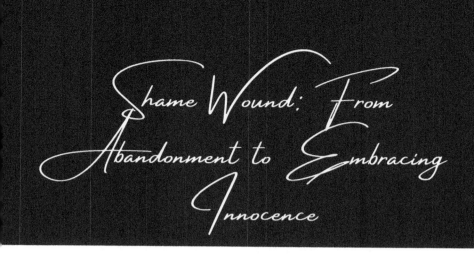

Shame Wound: From Abandonment to Embracing Innocence

"Shame is the lie someone told you about yourself." - Anaïs Nin

In the realm of human emotions, shame is a shapeshifter. Sometimes it's an insidious whisper, so faint you'd think it's the wind; at other times, it's a deafening roar that drowns out our inner truths. This feeling, so subtle and elusive, often acts as an anchor, preventing us from stepping into our authentic selves, establishing genuine boundaries, and truly seeing our worth.

Rejection is a powerful emotion. From the sting of being the last one picked in a school sports team to the chill of a distant parent's indifference, these moments create more than just memories. They carve deep gashes into our psyche. Now, imagine a sapling, young and fresh, trying to grow towards the sun. Each time it's stepped on or overshadowed, it bends a little, its growth hindered. Confused and hurt, it doesn't understand why it's being trampled, leading it to believe, "Maybe I don't deserve the sunlight." Combine this with experiences of neglect in our formative years or any form of abuse, and we're left with a potent cocktail of self-doubt and self-loathing: The Shame Wound. This, dear reader, is how the seed of this wound is sown.

The central belief weaving its way through the Shame Wound is that biting, aching feeling: "I am not worthy of love." It's like wearing a heavy cloak that weighs you down. But here's a secret: it's not your cloak. It was draped over you by circumstances and sometimes, by people who themselves were draped in their own cloaks of pain.

The individuals we allow into our lives can either respect or erode our boundaries. When guided by deep-seated shame, we might gravitate towards those who fail to respect us. On a subconscious level, these individuals confirm our misconstrued self-worth perceptions. But guess what? We have the power to break that cycle. The moment we recognize this pattern is the moment our healing truly begins.

When shame becomes unbearable, a defense mechanism is sometimes activated. In a bid to shake off this overwhelming weight, some might adopt narcissistic tendencies. It isn't a genuine reflection of self-worth but a desperate cry: "See me, validate me."

Pause for a moment! Before you're pulled into the whirlwind of despair, anchor yourself with this truth: every scar hides a potential for profound healing. To mend the Shame Wound is not just about patching up past hurts, but a journey towards embracing your inherent worth. Regardless of the shadows of past experiences, your true essence remains unblemished and deeply lovable. Rediscovering your innate innocence overwrites the entrenched beliefs of unworthiness.

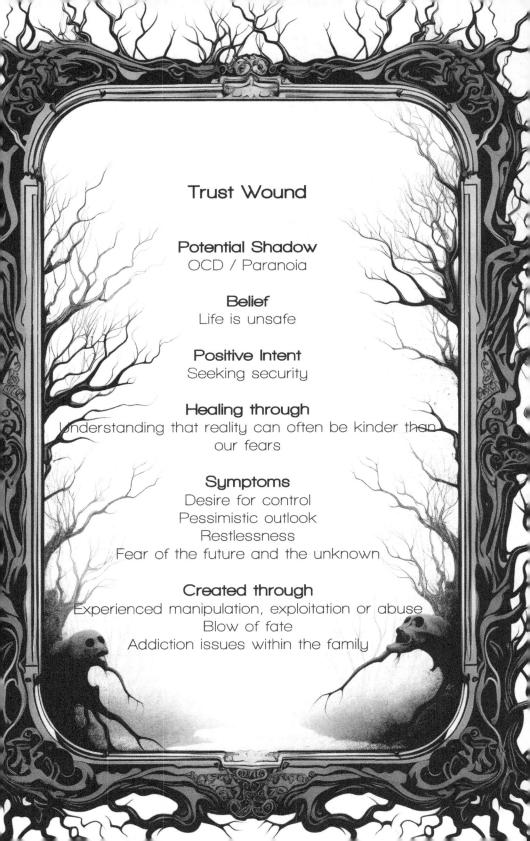

Trust Wound

Potential Shadow
OCD / Paranoia

Belief
Life is unsafe

Positive Intent
Seeking security

Healing through
Understanding that reality can often be kinder than our fears

Symptoms
Desire for control
Pessimistic outlook
Restlessness
Fear of the future and the unknown

Created through
Experienced manipulation, exploitation or abuse
Blow of fate
Addiction issues within the family

Trust Wound: A Journey from Fear to Faith

"To conquer fear is the beginning of wisdom."
— *Bertrand Russell*

Trust is such a delicate fabric, easily torn and tediously mended. Some of us have felt its fray too early, too harshly, and that has left behind what we call the Trust Wound. But just like any scar, it tells a story.

When we look closely, we notice certain behaviors in ourselves—like an obsessive need to double-check things or that eerie feeling that something's not right. Think of it as a silent alarm, signaling deeper issues. It's not just about being meticulous or cautious; it's a manifestation of deeper fears, echoing painful past experiences.

Remember that time when someone you trusted turned their back on you? Or when an unexpected event turned your life upside down? It's like the rug was pulled out from under your feet. And in those moments, a dangerous belief seeded itself within: that life, in all its unpredictability, is fundamentally unsafe.

This belief doesn't just stay dormant. It shows up in little ways—like the need to control every tiny aspect of our lives, expecting the worst out of situations, or that restless feeling, akin to waiting for a storm when the sky is clear.

It's the proverbial monster under our beds, only this one's in our minds, making us dread what tomorrow might bring.

But here's a perspective to ponder: What if we're haunted not by reality, but by the ghosts of 'What ifs'?

For those of us healing from the trust wound, the challenge is not about forgetting the past but shifting our lens towards the future. It's about retraining our brain to not always expect a thunderstorm. It's about letting in the possibility that the future can be radiant and welcoming.

While caution is a tool for survival, constantly living in its shadow means we're surviving, not thriving. Instead of always preparing for battles, what if we also prepared for celebrations? Instead of focusing on potential heartbreaks, why not also anticipate heartwarming moments?

It's essential to remind ourselves that fear, in its essence, is a story we tell ourselves. And if we have the power to script these tales of dread, we also possess the ability to rewrite them with hope, curiosity, and optimism.

Isn't it liberating to think that the future, in its vastness, holds as many opportunities as challenges? That for every potential setback, there's also a potential for a comeback?

So, let's embark on this transformative journey—from fear to faith, from skepticism to hope. It's time to heal, rediscover trust, and embrace the countless 'What ifs' that sparkle with positivity.

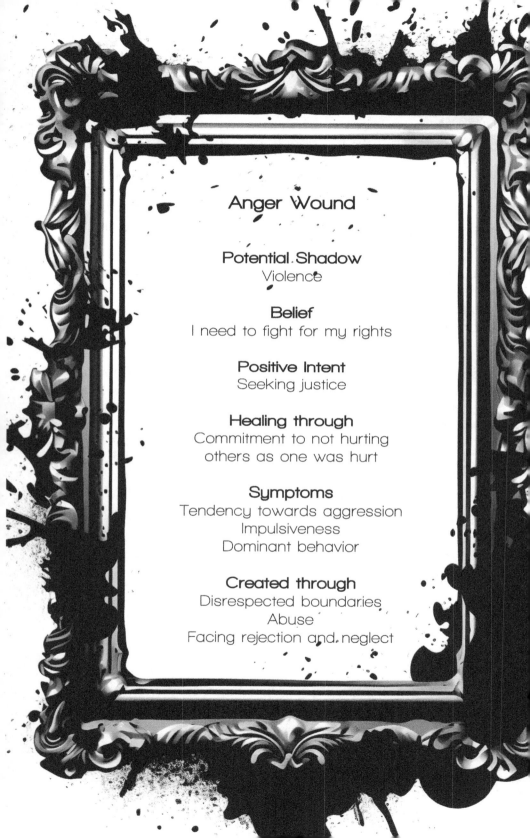

Anger Wound

Potential Shadow
Violence

Belief
I need to fight for my rights

Positive Intent
Seeking justice

Healing through
Commitment to not hurting
others as one was hurt

Symptoms
Tendency towards aggression
Impulsiveness
Dominant behavior

Created through
Disrespected boundaries
Abuse
Facing rejection and neglect

Anger Wound: From Force to Flow

'It's a lot easier to be angry at someone than it is to tell them you're hurt." - Tom Gates

When we think of anger, what usually comes to mind? Flaring tempers, raised voices, and maybe even the clenching of fists. But anger is not just an explosive emotion; it's a wound. It's a shadow that lurks in the corners of our hearts, often hidden, sometimes surfacing when we least expect it. And when it does, it brings with it a whirlwind of destruction and chaos.

Anger, at its root, is about violated boundaries and unmet expectations. When we feel disrespected, abused, neglected, or rejected, anger often rises as a defense mechanism. It tells a story of a time when our boundaries were crossed, leaving a scar that whispers, "I need to fight for my rights." There's a belief that fighting brings justice, that the fire of anger can forge the path to fairness.

But like any fire, anger can be both constructive and destructive. It can motivate us to change, push us out of complacency, or it can consume and destroy. When not harnessed correctly, this shadow can manifest as violence, and we become aggressive, impulsive, and dominant. We find ourselves using force, not to affirm life but to resist and fight against it, seeking an illusionary sense of power.

However, true power isn't about dominating others or demanding our way. It's about flowing harmoniously with life, finding strength in love and respect. The irony? In our desperate pursuit of control, the anger wound makes us believe we are powerful when, in fact, we are at our most vulnerable.

The wound of anger is deceptive. It wears many faces: impatience with a co-worker, frustration with life's circumstances, road rage, passive-aggressive comments, or even outright physical or verbal aggression. It feels intoxicating, even heroic at times. But at its core, it's an unresolved sadness, a child's tantrum, a desperate scream for love and recognition.

Every time our expectations aren't met, this wound gets a jolt, reminding us of the times we felt violated, disrespected, or unloved. It creates imaginary enemies, obstacles, and burdens. It convinces us that the world is against us, that everyone is a potential threat.

To truly heal, we need to recognize that anger's force is just a mask for underlying fear. We must let go of our entitlement, our attachment to results, and our desperate need for control. Instead, we should cultivate genuine self-esteem, find security within ourselves, and understand that true power comes from peace, love, and respect.

To navigate the turbulent waters of anger, we need to ground ourselves in a profound understanding of our inherent value. It's about recognizing our intrinsic worth, one that remains unswayed by the world around us. When you stand before the mirror each day, remind yourself, "I am cherished, I am grounded, and I have no need to assert control over all things."

When anger's flames threaten to consume you, pause for a beat. Let the breath anchor you. Understand that every heated word, every intense face-off, every surge of aggression is an invitation to introspect and heal. Heed that invitation. Because genuine strength doesn't lie in overpowering others; it's anchored in empathy, compassion, and mutual respect.

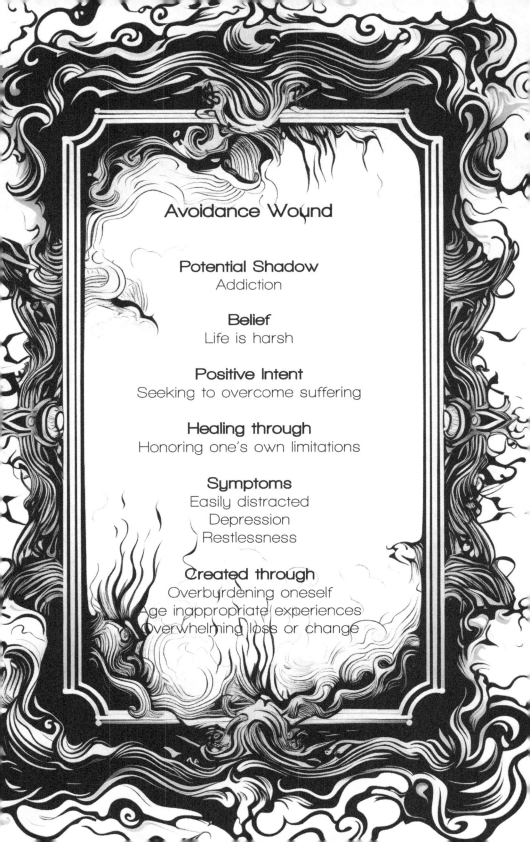

Avoidance Wound

Potential Shadow
Addiction

Belief
Life is harsh

Positive Intent
Seeking to overcome suffering

Healing through
Honoring one's own limitations

Symptoms
Easily distracted
Depression
Restlessness

Created through
Overburdening oneself
Age inappropriate experiences
Overwhelming loss or change

Avoidance Wound: Facing Life's Overwhelms Head-On

"We can run, but we can't hide from ourselves."
- Carl G. Jung

Have you ever felt like life was just too much? As if every single responsibility, every daunting task, every emotional burden was a mountain too steep to climb? If you've nodded in agreement, then you've felt the weight of what I'd call the 'Avoidance Wound'.

Picture this: you're handed far more than you can realistically handle, from expectations that soar beyond your reach to experiences that seem too mature for your age. Or maybe it's the paralyzing weight of unexpected change or loss that you never saw coming. When life relentlessly pummels us with such blows, it's as if our spirit decides, "Enough's enough. Let's pull the curtains and retreat." And the internal mantra becomes: Life is harsh.

This retreat isn't just a casual step back. It manifests in tangible ways. Distractions become the norm; anything to keep our minds off the real issues. Feelings of depression may seep in, and a restless itch takes root, prompting us to continuously seek escape. And in the darkest alleys of this wound? Addiction waits, ready to offer its false solace.

From the outside, this might sound like a bad case of pessimism, but it runs deeper. Overwhelm is akin to being buried under a pile of feelings, to-dos, regrets, and more. Everything appears pointless. Why bother trying? Why hope? Every possible solution is met with a desolate, "What's the point?" or "It's too late now."

And it's not just about daily responsibilities. Overwhelm can be triggered by deep-seated traumas or losses — the passing away of a loved one, the end of a cherished relationship, the memories of time wasted in negativity, or even tragic accidents that leave us feeling bereft and broken.

But here's where the silver lining peeks through. Every wound, no matter how deep, carries within it the seeds of healing. The key to mending the Avoidance Wound lies in two simple steps: accepting and seeking help.

You see, when we let ourselves truly feel, embracing even the heaviest of emotions, we begin our journey to healing. It's perfectly alright to grieve, to feel lost, or to break down. But once we've let these emotions wash over us, it's vital to reach out. Whether it's counseling, spiritual guidance, a chat with a friend, or simply a whispered prayer in the night, asking for help is a potent remedy.

There's a profound power in surrendering to our vulnerabilities, in admitting we're not okay, and in seeking a hand to guide us out of the darkness. It's about reframing our perception of loss and facing it head-on. Because, dear reader, just by inviting help, by allowing yourself to be open to guidance and change, you'll find your way out. And you're not alone in this. Miracles happen. New beginnings await. Hope is never truly lost.

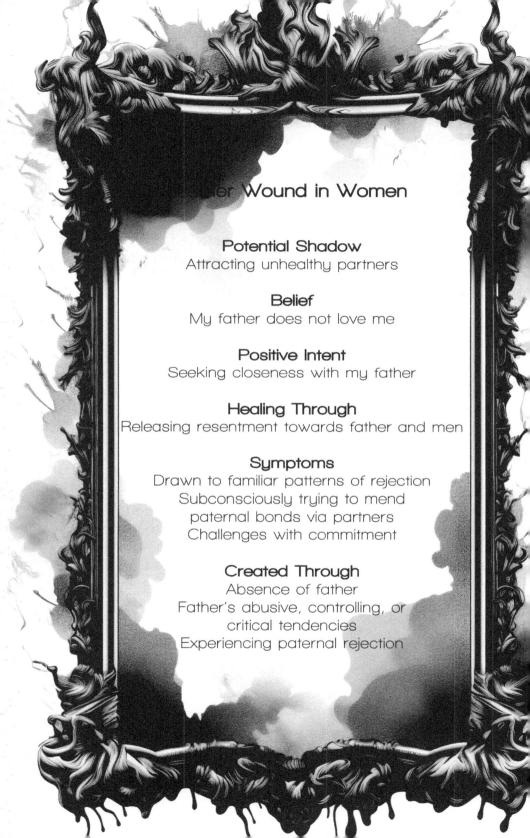

...er Wound in Women

Potential Shadow
Attracting unhealthy partners

Belief
My father does not love me

Positive Intent
Seeking closeness with my father

Healing Through
Releasing resentment towards father and men

Symptoms
Drawn to familiar patterns of rejection
Subconsciously trying to mend
paternal bonds via partners
Challenges with commitment

Created Through
Absence of father
Father's abusive, controlling, or
critical tendencies
Experiencing paternal rejection

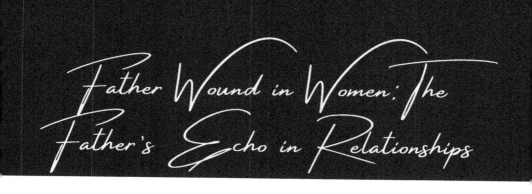

Father Wound in Women: The Father's Echo in Relationships

"The way we talk to our children becomes their inner voice."
- Peggy O'Mara

Imagine your heart as a magnetic compass, pointing toward your most profound desires and occasionally, the very dilemmas that riddle your journey. For many women, this compass seems to be magnetically drawn back to one figure: Daddy. Before you jump to conclusions, this isn't some clichéd narrative. It's an exploration into the intricacies of relationships, influenced significantly by early bonds.

Though we're focusing on the father-daughter dynamic, it's crucial to recognize that such emotional compasses are universally present across genders, orientations, and partner preferences. Whether it's a father-son, mother-daughter, mother-son, or any other parental-child dynamic, these deep-seated feelings and patterns manifest in myriad ways. This is the human experience, encompassing every shade and nuance of our relationships. After all, the need for love, acceptance, and understanding is universal, and we all navigate these waters in our unique ways.

When a father, a significant figure in a girl's life, is absent, critical, or even abusive, it's akin to a compass being thrown off its axis. Consequently, some women find themselves consistently attracting partners reminiscent of the pains experienced with their fathers. Think of it as a misfiring GPS, continuously rerouting back to the same heartache-laden path.

John Bowlby's groundbreaking work on attachment theory highlighted how our earliest bonds impact our adult relationships. When there's an unstable early attachment, like a tumultuous relationship with one's father, it can lay the blueprint for future relational patterns.

So, when a woman's relationship with her father was distant or challenging, it might sow the seeds of a debilitating belief: that she's not worthy of true affection. A voice might whisper from the shadows, "If even your father couldn't love you fully, how can another?" Yet, beneath this painful notion lies a profound yearning: the desire to rekindle closeness with a fatherly figure. It's this latent hope that might lead some women to choose partners with similar dynamics, in a subconscious bid to rectify the original relationship with their fathers.

Have you ever felt an inexplicable pull towards partners who embody all-too-familiar feelings of rejection? Or found commitment daunting, fearing it's just a prelude to yet another abandonment episode? These are the signs, the echoes of past pains clamoring for recognition and healing.

The silver lining? Nobody is preordained to remain ensnared in these patterns. To embark on a healing trajectory, consider:

Release Resentment: It's not about forgetting or even excusing. It's about liberating oneself from the shackles of bygone traumas. Releasing pent-up resentment towards one's father can herald a transformative personal evolution.

Reframe Beliefs: It's natural for past experiences, especially those with a father, to shape perceptions about other men. But remember, all men aren't the mold of one's father. Challenge those deeply embedded beliefs about men stemming from past experiences. Consider, "Not all men mirror my father's actions, and I am deserving of a relationship built on trust, respect, and unconditional love."

By acknowledging and reshaping these beliefs, one not only liberates themselves from past pains but also opens up the possibility of healthier relationships with men who offer genuine love and partnership.

It's essential to remember that while this chapter has highlighted five significant wounds, the spectrum of personal wounds can be broader. Everyone's shadow carries its unique patterns and pain points. While these insights serve as a foundation, it's crucial to have an open dialogue with your individual shadow and not to minimize its significance just because it may not have been explicitly discussed in this chapter.

As you navigated through the different wounds discussed in this chapter, which one resonated with you the most and why?

In your day-to-day life, are there specific triggers or situations that evoke feelings related to these wounds? How do you usually respond?

Envision a life where these wounds are healed. What does that look like for you? How would your daily experiences and interactions change?

What are the first steps you feel compelled to take towards that vision?

I am who I am and that is enough

CHAPTER TWO

Let the Inner Exploration begin: Shadow Work Essentials

How to Spot Your Shadow

"The most terrifying thing is to accept oneself completely." - Carl G. Jung

Envision yourself as Sherlock Holmes, the famed detective donned in his signature deerstalker hat. Your shadow is like Dr. Moriarty, cleverly hidden, but revealing itself in unexpected moments. Just as Sherlock always catches Moriarty, we're going to do the same with our shadow.

Overreaction – The Emotional Flare-ups

Ever snapped at someone for a minor thing? Or maybe you've been on the receiving end of someone's inexplicable anger? This might be the shadow at play. Our overreactions are often the outcome of unresolved emotional trauma or suppressed emotions. So, next time you feel that surge of emotion, instead of brushing it off, grab your metaphorical magnifying glass and delve deeper.

Projection – The World's a Mirror

If you've ever thought, "Why is everyone else so _____?", that blank might be a piece of your shadow. Often, the qualities we dislike in others are the ones we don't accept in ourselves. That colleague who's "too bossy" or the neighbor who's "always showing off" could mirror the traits you've suppressed.

Repetitive Patterns

Ever wondered, "Why does this always happen to me?" Be it relationships, jobs, or any recurring life situations – these patterns often have a shadowy root. They're the universe's way of pointing towards aspects we need to address.

Triggers and Defense Mechanisms

"Oh, I always avoid talking about that!" or "I usually make jokes when I feel uncomfortable." These are defense mechanisms that protect us from confronting our shadow. Any topic or situation that makes us uncomfortable or defensive might be holding a clue to our shadow. Embrace vulnerability. The next time you feel defensive, pause and ask yourself, "What am I protecting?"

Emotional Flare-ups: *Reflect on the last time you overreacted to a situation. Write down the specifics of what happened. What do you think might have been the deeper emotion or suppressed memory at play? How did you feel immediately after the event?*

Mirror, Mirror on the Wall: *List down three traits or behaviors you've recently observed in others that irked or bothered you. For each trait, write about a time you might have displayed that behavior or felt the urge to. What emotions arise as you reflect on this?*

Patterns in Play: *Think of a recurring event or pattern in your life. Describe it in detail. What emotions or thoughts do you associate with this repetitive cycle? If your shadow could speak through this pattern, what do you think it would say?*

Trigger Points & Shields: *Identify a topic or situation that you actively avoid or get defensive about. Dive into why it makes you uncomfortable. If you had to face this head-on, what's the worst and best thing that could happen?*

Starting a Conversation with Your Shadow

*"The cave you fear to enter
holds the treasure you seek."*
– *Joseph Campbell*

Alright, adventurers of the psyche, it's time to roll up our sleeves and get personal. Remember those whispers in your ear when you least expect them? That voice which seems to nudge you in unexpected ways? Yep, that's our shadow doing the talking. And guess what? It's high time we replied.

As with all the best conversations in life, start with an open heart. You wouldn't snap at a dear friend before they've even spoken, right? Your shadow, despite the somewhat ominous name, isn't some arch-villain. It's a piece of you. Treat it as you would an old friend you've lost touch with. Yes, there might be awkward pauses and hesitant starts, but oh, the stories it has to tell!

The shadow is born from our experiences. Every time we were told "big boys don't cry" or "good girls stay quiet", parts of us were pushed into the shadows. This suppression wasn't out of malice; often it was a protection mechanism, keeping our fragile selves from heartbreak, rejection, or shame. Recognize that your shadow's formation wasn't about being 'bad' or 'wrong'. It was simply coping.

This isn't an interrogation. No harsh lights and pressing demands. The shadow, after being hidden for so long, might be wary. After all, it's seen the sharp end of suppression and rejection. Approach it with gentleness, understanding, and patience. It's not about prying open locked doors but waiting for them to be opened from the inside.

As you delve deeper, you'll find moments of revelation. Why you bristle at certain comments, why specific songs stir a whirlwind of emotions, or why certain scents take you back decades. It's a journey of unraveling and understanding. And, every step of the way, you're not alone; you're in the best company—yourself.

Think of the countless moments in your day where your mind drifts off just a bit—while waiting for your coffee to brew, taking a brief walk, or even during those idle moments in a shower. These moments aren't reserved solely for grand revelations or epic soul-searching sessions. Instead, they offer a chance to weave an ongoing dialogue with your shadow into the very fabric of your day-to-day life. The magic truly lies in this integration into everyday experiences. By consistently inviting your shadow into these simple moments, you're making a conscious effort to bridge the gap between the conscious and unconscious realms of your psyche. The goal is to foster a continuous thread of communication, ensuring you're always tuned in and receptive to its insights, whether it's hinting at a forgotten memory or signaling an old wound.

Making this dialogue with your shadow an integral part of your daily life doesn't just lead to fleeting moments of insight— it paves the way for deep-seated transformation. The more you practice this, the more profound your understanding and bond with that once-hidden part of yourself becomes. It's not just about acknowledging the shadow but about truly merging with it, allowing its wisdom to shape your responses, choices, and overall outlook. This is where the biggest shifts happen. Not in isolated introspective sessions, but in the consistent, day-by-day merging of the shadow with the conscious self. The result? A more harmonized, authentic, and enlightened version of you.

Journaling Prompts: Start a Conversation with Your Shadow

First Words: *If you could say one thing to your shadow right now, what would it be? And what might it reply?*

Listening Practice: *Spend a few quiet moments today simply listening, without judgment. What does your shadow wish you knew?*

Open-Ended Queries: *Ask your shadow, "What have I been ignoring?" Journal the first thoughts that come to mind.*

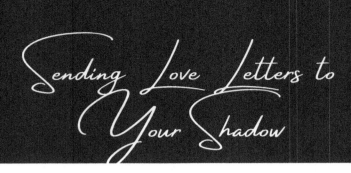

Sending Love Letters to Your Shadow

"The meeting of two personalities is like the contact of two chemical substances: if there is any reaction, both are transformed."
– Carl G. Jung

Ding! You've got mail! But wait, this isn't your regular kind of letter. It's intimate, personal, and transformative. Think of it as the warmest, fuzziest, most soul-touching message you could send to yourself.

Now, you might be asking, "Why on Earth would I write a love letter to my shadow?" Stick with me here! Think back to the last time you received a heartfelt letter. The rush of warmth, the twinkle in your eye, the immediate connection to the sender. Now imagine directing all those fuzzy feelings inward, towards the parts of you that have been yearning for that love and attention.

Alright, pen and paper (or keyboard) at the ready! The best letters aren't the ones that have been drafted and redrafted a gazillion times. They're raw, real, and sometimes, they come with a few hilarious typos (or tear smudges). Start by acknowledging your shadow. Say "Hey there!" or "Long time no chat!". Apologize if you've been giving it the cold shoulder and express your eagerness to reconnect.

As you pen down your feelings, get specific. Remember that time you felt a pang of jealousy at a friend's success? Or when you snapped unexpectedly at a loved one? Yep, those were shadowy moments! Mention these instances, thank your shadow for the lessons, and share your thoughts on them. It's all about getting personal.

We all love promises, especially the ones we can keep! So, in your love-filled note, make some heartfelt commitments to your shadow. Maybe you promise to listen more, or perhaps, you pledge not to run away from those uncomfortable feelings. Whatever it is, make sure it's something you can stick to.

Remember the thrill of awaiting a letter from a pen pal? Your shadow's no different. It's eager for more! This isn't just a one-time affair; keep the conversation going. Whether you set aside a monthly "shadow date" or randomly jot down thoughts when the mood strikes, stay connected.

This is more than just a letter-writing exercise. It's a profound journey of self-discovery and love. By expressing warmth, understanding, and a sprinkle of fun to your shadow, you're building bridges to the most secluded parts of yourself. So, keep those letters coming, and who knows? Your shadow might just pen one back!

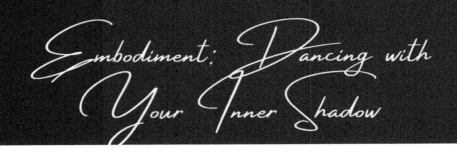
Embodiment: Dancing with Your Inner Shadow

"The body says what words cannot."
- Martha Graham

Have you ever tried learning a new dance? Initially, you're all feet and no rhythm, and every move feels foreign, like you're wrapped in cling film trying to break free. That's a lot like getting in touch with the deeper parts of ourselves. This chapter, dear reader, is all about dancing with our inner shadows, discovering our true rhythm, and embodying our most authentic self. Buckle up, it's going to be a jazzy ride!

The Power of Presence

Imagine for a moment that your body is a beautifully designed instrument. Every part, from your fingertips to your toes, resonates with its unique sound. Yet, often, we're too caught up in our heads, lost in thoughts of yesterday's regrets or tomorrow's anxieties, to truly listen.

Try This Out: Find a quiet space and sit comfortably. Take deep breaths, feeling the air fill your lungs and the weight of your body grounded. Begin to listen to your heartbeat, feel the sensations in your hands, and observe the subtle energy that flows through you. This exercise isn't about achieving some zen state. It's simply about being present and feeling alive, right here, right now.

Embracing Your Inner Shadow

Our shadows aren't always about darkness and hidden fears. They can also be talents, passions, and dreams we've tucked away, thinking they weren't 'appropriate' or 'achievable'. Guess what? It's time to shed some light on them! Think of something you've always loved doing, but pushed to the backburner for some reason. Maybe you adored painting as a child but dropped it because adulting got in the way.

Somatic Experience: Tapping into Body Wisdom

Our bodies hold memories, emotions, and truths that our minds might often overlook or suppress. A practice called 'somatic experiencing' helps in tapping into this body wisdom to heal traumas and rediscover our authenticity.

Activity: Standing or sitting comfortably, start by shaking out each limb individually. Feel the energy release. Then, move your body in ways it wants to, without judgment. Maybe it's swaying your hips or just rotating your ankles. The key is to let your body guide you, not the other way around.

Walking the Talk

It's one thing to have insights about our shadows, and quite another to embody them in our daily lives. It's like knowing the dance steps but never actually dancing. Time to hit the dance floor of life!

Challenge: Over the next week, pick one insight or realization you've had about your shadow side. Now, embody it. If you discovered a suppressed passion for singing, maybe you can take a singing lesson or have a solo karaoke night. Whatever it is, make it real. Dance with your shadow, not away from it.

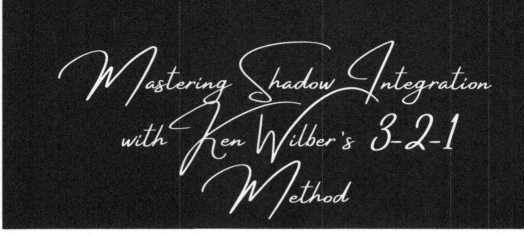

Mastering Shadow Integration with Ken Wilber's 3-2-1 Method

"The shadow exists only as unsymbolized
thoughts, feelings, sensations, and behaviors.
When they are all symbolized and integrated,
the shadow 'disappears' and only the Self
remains."
- Ken Wilber

Alright, lovely readers, here comes the magic trick for transforming those shadowy parts of you! You've delved into the depths, faced those daunting parts, and now? Now it's time to integrate. And how do you do that? Enter the 3-2-1 Method by Ken Wilber. It's as easy as, well, 3-2-1!

The Third-Person Perspective (3)

Start by thinking of your shadow aspect as 'it'—like it's a character in a book or a movie. Describe it. What does it look like? Sound like? How does it behave? By seeing your shadow as an 'it', you create a bit of distance. This gives you a chance to observe without getting emotionally entangled.

For instance: Instead of "I am always so angry," consider "There's a part of me that carries this anger."

The Second-Person Perspective (2)

Now, let's get a little personal. Address this shadow aspect as 'you'. Engage with it in a dialogue. Ask questions. Why are you here? What do you want? By treating your shadow as a 'you', you start building a relationship with it.

Imagine saying: "Hey Anger, why did you flare up during that meeting today?"

The First-Person Perspective (1)

Finally, it's time to fully embrace and own this part of yourself. This is where you refer to your shadow as 'I'. Feel it. Understand it. Befriend it. When you fully integrate it, it's no longer something you fight against but a part of who you are. Think: "I understand why I felt that anger. It's a part of me, and I am learning from it."

Now, a gentle reminder: this dance with your shadow is delicate, and it demands patience. This isn't a race. You don't need to leap from one perspective to the next in haste. In fact, consider luxuriating in each stage for a day or so. Allow the insights to simmer, the revelations to marinate. Be tender with yourself, granting the kindness and time you deserve. Because true self-understanding isn't a sprint; it's a lifelong, beautiful marathon.

Reflecting the Shadow:
The Mirror Technique

"Everything that irritates us about others can lead us to an understanding of ourselves." - Carl G. Jung

Ever caught your reflection in a mirror and wondered, "Is that really how I look?" Now, let's turn that physical reflection into a deeper, psychological one. The Mirror Technique is about using the external world as a, well, mirror, to identify, acknowledge, and heal the shadow parts of ourselves.

Identify Reflections

Think of instances where you had strong reactions to someone else's behavior, whether positive or negative. These reactions are often your unconscious mind pointing towards a trait you possess but might not be fully aware of.

Example: Feeling a strong dislike for a colleague's arrogant demeanor.

Self-Reflection

Ask yourself why you felt so strongly about that behavior. What does it reveal about your own beliefs, values, or suppressed traits?

Question: "Why does his arrogance bother me so much? Do I secretly crave the confidence he displays? Or am I suppressing a similar trait in myself?"

Own and Integrate

If you identify a suppressed trait, own it. This doesn't mean acting out but acknowledging its existence. Then, think of healthy ways to express or channel this trait.

Action: "I recognize I too have a confident side I've suppressed fearing it might come off as arrogance. I'll focus on expressing my opinions more assertively in meetings."

Gratitude for the Mirror

Every person or situation that triggers a strong emotion in you is offering you a chance to introspect and grow. Express gratitude for these mirrors in your life.

Mental Note: "Thank you, colleague, for unconsciously helping me recognize and integrate a part of my shadow."

By constantly observing our reactions and what they reveal about us, the Mirror Technique offers a direct pathway to not only recognize our shadows but also to embrace and integrate them in a constructive manner.

Reflection on Resonance: *Which technique(s) felt just right or spoke to you most deeply? Why?*

Mapping the Journey: *How do you envision incorporating your chosen technique(s) into your daily or weekly rhythm?*

I am who I am and that is enough

Free Shadow Work Meditation

Embark on a meditation journey that goes beyond mere contemplation—it's a deep, interactive exchange with your shadow self. Delve into its depths, guided at each turn, to not just witness but actively converse with your innermost layers. This isn't your everyday meditation; it's an enlightening chat with the unsung parts of you.

Ready to start this introspective dialogue? Dive in at felixbuchwald.com/meditation or simply scan the QR code below.

Get to know your Shadow

SHADOW WORK MEDITATION

ACCESS FOR FREE AT
FELIXBUCHWALD.COM/MEDITATION

CHAPTER THREE

Alphabet of the Heart: Emotions are Your Soul's Language

Introduction

"The heart has its own language. The heart knows a hundred thousand ways to speak."
– Rumi

The heart has its own dialect. It speaks in hushed whispers, jubilant shouts, and a range of tones in between. Its alphabet is emotion, its grammar is experience, and its vocabulary is vast.

Introduction: Speaking Heart-ese

Have you ever been so overtaken by a feeling that words fell short to describe it? Maybe it was the overwhelming elation from an unexpected compliment or that twinge in your gut when something didn't feel quite right. I like to think of these moments as the heart speaking its unique language. A language so pure and powerful, it's not bound by any lexicon. This is your soul's way of communicating with you.

Why Emotions Are the Alphabet of the Heart

Imagine a child, learning to speak. They'll first grasp at sounds, then words, and finally, sentences. Our emotions work similarly. Each feeling, be it joy, sadness, anger, or contentment, is a letter in the heart's alphabet. And just like a child's vocabulary grows with experience, so does our emotional depth.

Favorites & Uninvited Guests

We all have favorites, don't we? Ice cream flavors, movie genres, and yes, emotions. We yearn for joy, love, and exhilaration. They're like the hit tracks on our life's playlist. And then there are those we often wish to skip—sadness, pain, or jealousy. The thing is, in the language of the heart, every emotion is a crucial word. Picking and choosing emotions is like cherry-picking words from a language and expecting to still understand the complete story.

Emotions and Relationships: The Perfect Analogy

Imagine you're in a relationship (with a partner, a friend, or a family member). If they constantly asked for your help with a task and you consistently ignored them, what would happen? Your bond would weaken, misunderstandings would arise, and the relationship would eventually sour.

Now, let's relate this to our relationship with our emotions. If you constantly ignore sadness or evade anger, you're essentially telling parts of yourself, "You don't matter." Over time, these ignored or suppressed emotions become shadows, lurking and yearning for attention.

Finding Equanimity

The concept of equanimity is about maintaining a mental calmness and even-temperedness, especially in difficult situations. When we view emotions as a language, equanimity becomes our translator. It teaches us to listen to the full spectrum of our heart's dialect without bias.

Unlocking the Shadows with Emotion

Now, I want you to think of Shadow Work as a passionate letter exchange between your conscious and subconscious. It's juicy, dramatic, enlightening, and sometimes heartbreaking. By acknowledging and understanding these emotional letters, you're effectively unlocking the shadows that may be holding you back.

Here's how to start:

Acknowledge All Emotions: Don't shush or belittle any emotion. Welcome each one like a guest in your home.

Seek Understanding: When confronted with a challenging emotion, instead of running away, ask, "Why are you here? What message do you bring?"

Respond with Love: Even the most painful emotions are seeking love and acknowledgment. Treat them with the same compassion you'd offer to a loved one.

Decoding Emotions

"Feelings or emotions are the universal language and are to be honored. They are the authentic expression of who you are at your deepest place." – Judith Wright

LOVE – WE ARE ONE

JOY – I'M TRULY ALIVE

SADNESS – I MISS A CONNECTION

ANGER – THIS ISN'T OKAY!

JEALOUSY – I DESIRE THAT TOO

FEAR – THIS ISN'T FOR ME

GUILT – I AIM HIGHER

SHAME – I EXPECT MORE OF MYSELF

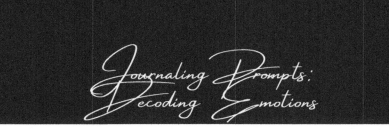

Journaling Prompts:
Decoding Emotions

Reflect on your recent feelings and identify the emotion that stands out the most to you.

Considering that every emotion conveys a message, does this perspective alter how you relate to the emotion you've identified? If so, in what ways?

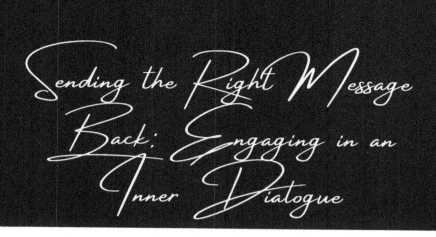

Sending the Right Message Back: Engaging in an Inner Dialogue

"One must talk to oneself, and for oneself. This produces a dialogue, and out of that dialogue one makes up one's mind." - Jiddu Krishnamurti

So, you've just cracked the code to the secret messages your emotions have been dispatching. But now what? Understanding their chatter is step one, but hey, real growth happens when you engage in some heart-to-heart conversations with them.

The Embrace of Acceptance

When Sadness murmurs, "I miss them" it doesn't necessarily want you to dive headfirst into a sea of despair. It's a soft tug at your heartstrings, a reminder. Start by acknowledging its presence without judgment. Give it a warm embrace, and you may find it softens, making way for clarity.

Constructive Responses

Anger might flare up, declaring, "My space was crossed!" Instead of lashing out or bottling it up, consider using it as an alert system. What boundaries were crossed? How can you fortify or communicate them better? Use this as an opportunity to learn and assert yourself.

Positive Reinforcement

When Love whispers, "Our souls intertwine" it's more than just a warm fuzzy feeling. It's a call to action—to appreciate, cherish, and cultivate the bonds you share. Take a moment to express gratitude or perform an act of kindness. Small gestures can reverberate profoundly.

Seek Reflection, Not Suppression

If Jealousy nudges you saying, "I should have that!" don't push it aside. It's a compass pointing to perhaps a forgotten dream or aspiration. Instead of feeling down about it, reflect. Why do you feel this way? What steps can you take to bridge the gap between where you are and where you'd like to be?

Daily Dialogues

Make it a habit to engage in regular inner dialogues. It's like catching up with a dear friend. Sometimes, a simple check-in can provide profound insights. Understand their origins, respect their messages, and integrate their wisdom.

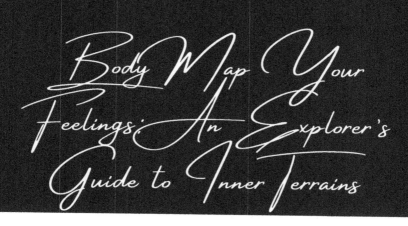

Body Map Your Feelings: An Explorer's Guide to Inner Terrains

"The body never lies." - Martha Graham

Embark with me on a captivating journey through the vast landscape of your body. Have you ever experienced those fluttering sensations in your stomach before a significant event? Or the heightened pulse when someone special walks by? It's more than just digestive whims or caffeine surges; our emotions have an innate tendency to express themselves physically.

Let's start with the body's intuitive center: the gut. Ever had a profound "I just know" sensation deep within, which later proved accurate? Some have dubbed the gut our 'second brain'. So, the next time you sense an emotional whirlwind in your stomach, pause and reflect. Perhaps it's a hint of apprehension for tomorrow's meeting?

Now, consider the heart. It's the perpetual rhythm of our existence. Anxious? It accelerates, echoing your inner turmoil. But on a serene day, it pulsates calmly, syncing with your peace. And during those poignant, tearful moments, each heartbeat resonates with profound emotion.

Moving on to the shoulders — the silent bearers of our burdens. Ever noticed how they tense up, especially during trying times? The next time that happens, visualize shedding a heavy load, a symbolic release of past regrets. It's an almost immediate route to relaxation.

Descend to the feet, our natural barometers. They might tap energetically to a lively tune or hint at impending nerves. They're both our rhythmic partners and our anchors to the world.

And then there are the hands. These versatile communicators often give away more than we realize. Under stress, they might clench, a vestige from our primal instincts. But in these moments, gently unfurl your fingers, letting go of accumulated tension, inviting a sense of calm.

In essence, our body is more than just a collection of reflexes. It's a symphony of signals, all intertwined, resonating with emotions and experiences. Every so often, take a moment to tune in. From your head to your toes, listen to the narratives they share. Perhaps even document these tales, creating your personalized emotional atlas. By tuning into and understanding our body's narratives, we unlock a profound dimension of self-awareness.

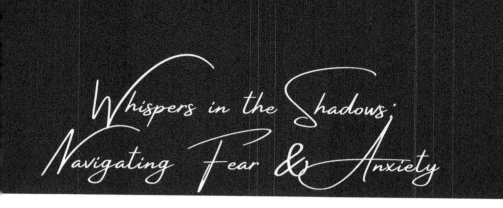

Whispers in the Shadows: Navigating Fear & Anxiety

"Fear keeps us focused on the past or worried about the future. If we can acknowledge our fear, we can realize that right now we are okay."
— Thich Nhat Hanh

Okay, picture this: you're navigating the maze-like alleys of a mysterious ancient city. Every corner you turn, there's a signpost named fear or anxiety, sometimes both, flashing neon and spewing fog. They're like those pesky pop-up ads on your browser – dramatic, a tad annoying, but still kind of serving a purpose.

Back in the day (and I mean way, way back), our ancestors were out there, making their way through the wild. A rustling in the bushes? Better believe they'd get their groove on and sprint in the other direction! Now, replace that rustling with unread emails, and you get the modern-day equivalent. Understanding this helps us give a nod to fear and anxiety, saying, "Hey, thanks for looking out!"

Now, have you ever heard the story of the man who believed he saw a snake in the dark, only to discover by daylight that it was merely a rope? Classic mix-up, right? But it paints a clear picture. Sometimes, our minds, after binge-watching their own series of past traumas and 'what-ifs', might see drama where there's nada. Anxiety can be that sneaky movie director, turning simple ropes into blockbuster serpents. But here's the twist: not every fear is just a rerun of an old movie. Sometimes, it's your inner compass gently saying, "This path? Not the right fit for us." Discerning true alarms from mere reverberations of the past? That, indeed, is the key.

Caught in a whirlwind of panic? Let's do a quick grounding game.

See: Spot 5 things around you.

Touch: Feel 4 objects within your reach.

Hear: Identify 3 distinct sounds.

Smell: Sniff out 2 different scents.

Taste: Notice any taste in your mouth. Can you pinpoint it?

This check-in acts like your mind's remote control, hitting the pause button on the chaos movie and landing you back in the present moment.

Navigating our emotional landscape, have you noticed where fear and anxiety usually take center stage? Perhaps it's that subtle palpitation in your chest or the sudden goosebumps waltzing on your arm. By attuning ourselves to these signals, we gain backstage access to the concert of our emotions. It becomes a quest to discern whether these feelings are here to orchestrate the main event or merely to add a distinctive touch.

As we navigate the intricate dance of fear and anxiety, we unearth hidden melodies. These emotions, when viewed beyond their initial intensity, can enrich our personal symphony, adding depth, resonance, and a narrative arc. So, as we move to the rhythm of life, recall: every emotion, including fear and anxiety, plays its part. Embrace it, learn from it, and dance onward.

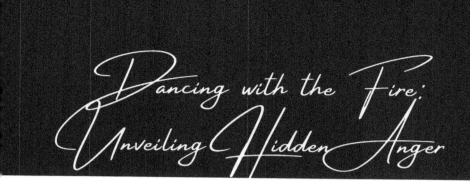

Dancing with the Fire: Unveiling Hidden Anger

"Speak when you are angry – and you'll make the best speech you'll ever regret."
- Laurence J. Peter

Alright, let's dive into the passionate tango of anger. Imagine being at a masquerade ball, and in waltzes Anger, wearing a vibrant mask, feathers flaring. Most guests might be a tad wary, whispering, "Who invited them?" But what if we shifted our lens? Picture anger not as the party crasher, but as the one who passionately cares about the house rules and wants to ensure everyone's having a good time. Anger is here, lighting up the dance floor, when someone steps on our toes or tries to change our favorite song. Ready to dance?

Flashback to our ancestors, hustling in the wild terrains without the niceties we take for granted. For them, anger was like that reliable watchtower guard, always on the lookout, alerting everyone, "Hey! That's not on!" By appreciating where anger's coming from, we can high-five it even in our most heated moments, saying, "Thanks for having my back!"

But hey, anger's got style—it doesn't always shout. Sometimes it's the quiet, sulky guest in the corner, the sarcastic toast, or the quick exit from an awkward chat. It loves costumes: one moment it's the diva named Irritation, the next, the mysterious figure of Passive Aggression.

Knowing its many guises makes our dance smoother and way more fun.

Underneath anger's flaming gown often lie delicate feelings, maybe even a few tears. Hidden are the heartaches, the dashed hopes, or those niggling insecurities. So, the next time anger flares up, maybe offer it a comforting drink and ask, "What's really going on?" Prepare to be surprised.

Recall our discussion on the emotional toolkit? Anger, that fervent performer, craves acknowledgment. Channel its intensity into a reflective journal entry, an earnest conversation with a trusted friend, or perhaps an uninhibited dance session in your living room. The goal? Expressing it with grace, ensuring it doesn't trigger any alarms.

Now, when anger seems ready to set the ballroom ablaze, it's grounding time! I like to think of it as the cool-down session after a fiery dance. Imagine anger transforming, going from blazing flamenco to a gentle waltz, until it takes a bow and merges with the crowd. You've got the moves, and with them, the power to change the tempo.

Often, anger just wants to set some party rules. It's telling us, "Hey, mark your dance space!" But it's not about shutting everyone out; it's about ensuring everyone grooves in harmony.

Embarking on this fiery dance with anger, we learn, twirl, and sometimes, stumble. But with a bit of rhythm and a lot of heart, we can turn it into the most exhilarating dance of our lives. So, as we strut forward, remember: every emotion, including our dance partner Anger, has its unique beat. Let's embrace it, sway with it, and most importantly, enjoy the party!

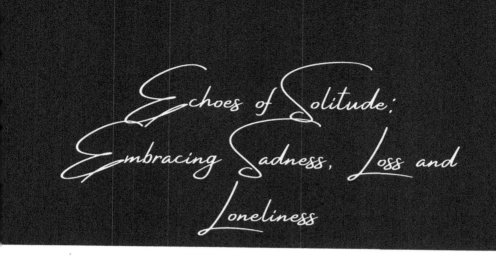

Echoes of Solitude: Embracing Sadness, Loss and Loneliness

"There is a sacredness in tears. They are not the mark of weakness, but of power. They are the messengers of overwhelming grief and unspeakable love." - Washington Irving

Navigating the tangled paths of sadness and loneliness can sometimes feel like trying to find your way through a room of funhouse mirrors—everything's a bit distorted, with each reflection pulling at your heartstrings in unexpected ways. Imagine if those emotions were songs. They'd probably be those soulful ballads that make you want to sway and reflect, all while munching on your favorite comfort food.

Our ancestors were a buddy-buddy bunch, sticking close together not just for the latest gossip by the campfire but because being alone was, quite literally, risky business. Fast-forward to today, and even with our smartphones practically attached to our hands, that ancient feeling of "Uh-oh, I'm alone!" still taps us on the shoulder now and then.

Ah, sadness. It's like that artist with a palette of blues, crafting our experiences with shades from baby blue disappointments to deep navy grief. And speaking of grief, if sadness were a foggy day, then processing loss is like trying to find your way through a particularly thick, pea-soup kind of mist. The kind where everything's blurry, but there's also a kind of quiet magic as you discover your inner compass.

But hang on a sec—before we dive too deep into the blues, let's tip our hats to solitude. Think of it as the cozy treehouse of emotions, nestled among the tallest trees. It's where you can snuggle up with a warm blanket, all while binging on your favorite series or getting lost in a book. It's alone time, but with a sprinkle of magic.

Here's the cool thing about sadness, loneliness, and those moments when you feel like you've misplaced your emotional map: They're like your personal GPS, signaling, "Hey, maybe it's time to call up that old friend!" or "How about reliving some sweet memories?" They're not nagging; they're gently suggesting routes toward healing and connection.

When these emotions start feeling like they've overstayed their welcome, imagine them as waves. Rather than getting caught in the undertow, stand your ground. Let each wave pass, knowing that every retreat carves out a bit more strength, wisdom, and, believe it or not, a sense of humor in your soul.

Life, with all its twists and turns, stitches together moments of sorrow, solitude, and loss, crafting a tapestry that's uniquely yours. Amid these threads, there's room to weave in vibrant stories of hope, love, and the next epic adventure.

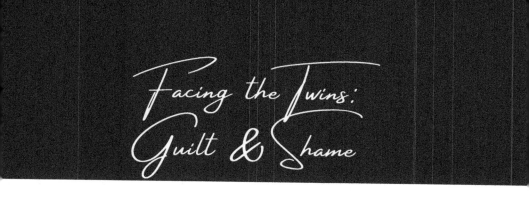

Facing the Twins: Guilt & Shame

"Shame corrodes the very part of us that
believes we are capable of change."
– Brené Brown

Alright, let's dive into a scene again. Imagine yourself back
at a swanky masquerade ball where you already met
the fiery anger. The room is dim, and masks glint with
every turn. In one corner, you spot two figures, their allure
undeniable. Meet Guilt and Shame. Now, they might come
across as that duo you'd love to avoid at a party, but
lean in closer, and you'll find they're the soul of the soirée,
carrying secrets worth uncovering.

Picture Guilt as the guest who accidentally steps on your
toes while dancing but is quick to apologize. That pang you
feel when you binge on cookies and then remember your
ignored gym membership? That's Guilt nudging you with a
reminder of your health goals. It's not about dwelling on that
misstep but a gentle push towards doing better next time.
Think of it as your favorite upbeat song—a reminder to find
your rhythm once again.

Now, waltzing deeper into the dance floor is Shame. This
one doesn't just look at your dance moves but questions
the very essence of your dance. While guilt highlights the
step you missed, shame wonders if you're even meant to
dance. The difference? Guilt focuses on the action, while
shame delves into identity. But here's the magic – the way
you engage with Shame defines its influence. Instead of

letting it dictate your worth, get curious. What's causing this deep resonance? By understanding its origins, you transform this slow ballad into a tune of empowerment.

So, now that you've mingled with these intriguing guests, how do you groove without getting your toes stepped on? First, spot that emotional twinge. What's it saying? Guilt or Shame? Then, dig deeper. What sparked it? Maybe an old memory or a recent event? And here's where the fun begins. Chat with these emotions as you would with a fellow dancer. Offer a reassuring nod, a comforting touch. Remember, they're not here to ruin the party but to add depth to your dance.

As the night rolls on, you realize Guilt and Shame aren't there to dim your sparkle but to refine your moves. So, when they approach, don't shy away. Take their hand, twirl, dip, and let the dance of self-discovery begin.

The Garden of Growth: Insecurity and Self-Worth

"You yourself, as much as anybody in the entire universe, deserve your love and affection."
- Buddha

If you've ever tried gardening, even just potting a plant, you'll agree it's not just about the plants. It's about the soil, the sunshine, the care, and sometimes, the sneaky weeds that pop up when you're not looking. Our inner world, darling reader, is not so different.

Picture this: Your mind as this sprawling garden. You've got your majestic trees – those are your big wins, your strengths. Then there are these brilliant blooms of joy and passion. But, hey, what's a garden without some drama? Enter the weeds of Insecurity and Lack of Self-Worth.

Insecurity is that vine that, left unchecked, can wrap around your blooming roses. It's sneaky, always whispering, "Are you sure about that? Do they really like you?" But here's the plot twist: Insecurity, with its sneaky tendrils, isn't all bad. When acknowledged, it might just point out where you need a bit more sun or water, metaphorically speaking. Dive into its roots, ask, "What's eating you, dear vine?" You might just find a pocket of your garden that's been thirsting for attention.

Then we have the bush of Lack of Self-Worth. A bit thorny, this one. It sits there, sometimes making you feel more hedgehog than human. But within, oh within, are the buds of your true value, waiting to bloom. Those prickles? They're just challenges, tests of resilience guarding the precious core of you. Nurture this bush, approach it with care, and remind yourself: I am worthy of every drop of sun and rain.

Gardening, like soul-searching, takes work. It demands patience, introspection, and yes, occasionally dealing with bugs and weeds. But that's the beauty of it. Every challenge, every weed, is just an invitation to grow, to adapt, to flourish even more radiantly.

A little tip from one gardener to another: When those weeds start to feel too wild, take a moment. Feel the sun on your face, appreciate the blooms you've cultivated, and the sturdy trees you've grown. You're not just a gardener; you're the heart of this verdant paradise.

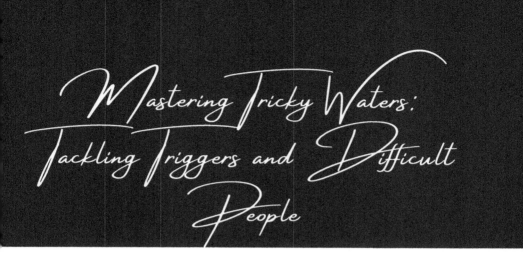

Mastering Tricky Waters: Tackling Triggers and Difficult People

*"Difficulties are meant to rouse, not discourage.
The human spirit is to grow strong by conflict."*
– William Ellery Channing

In the realm of understanding and transforming emotions, one essential skill is identifying your triggers. Triggers are like road signs pointing to underlying emotions, guiding you toward self-awareness and growth. By recognizing these triggers, you gain the power to navigate your emotional landscape with finesse. Let's delve into the process of identifying triggers and explore how to master interactions, even with the most challenging of personalities.

The Source of Ripples

Triggers are often hidden beneath the surface, waiting for a catalyst to stir them. Reflect on past experiences that evoked strong emotional responses. What circumstances or words led to these reactions? Recognizing the underlying triggers can be like illuminating the path ahead.

Mapping Your Emotional Terrain

Imagine creating a mental map of your emotional landscape. As you identify triggers, you draw lines connecting them to specific emotions. Over time, patterns emerge, helping you understand your triggers' origins and the emotional currents they create.

Responding with Intention

Challenging interactions can be like navigating uncharted waters. Instead of reacting impulsively, focus on responding with intention. Take a deep breath, allowing yourself a moment to consider your response. This practice empowers you to engage thoughtfully, even in the heat of the moment.

Cultivating Inner Resilience

Building resilience is like strengthening the hull of a ship—it helps you weather storms. Engage in practices that nurture your emotional well-being. Whether it's mindfulness, journaling, or seeking support from loved ones, these practices fortify your emotional anchor.

Mastering the Dance of Communication

Interacting with difficult personalities requires finesse. Approach these interactions as a dance—a mutual exchange. Practice active listening, empathy, and asserting your boundaries with grace. Remember, every interaction offers a chance to grow and learn.

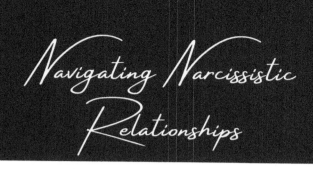
"The scars from mental cruelty can be as deep and long-lasting as wounds from punches or slaps but are often not as obvious."
- Lundy Bancroft

In the vast garden of human connections, we occasionally encounter a unique and challenging variety of personality: the narcissist. Navigating relationships with narcissistic individuals can feel like treading through a dense thicket—fraught with complexities and emotional obstacles. Yet, armed with understanding and strategies, you can cultivate resilience and protect your well-being.

Understanding the Narcissistic Spectrum

Narcissism isn't a one-size-fits-all trait. It exists on a spectrum, from mild to severe. Recognize the signs of narcissistic behavior, such as an inflated sense of self-importance, a constant need for admiration, and a lack of empathy. Understanding where an individual falls on this spectrum can guide your approach.

Setting Boundaries and Prioritizing Self-Care

Like erecting protective fences around delicate plants, setting boundaries is essential when dealing with narcissists. Clearly communicate your limits and priorities. Prioritize self-care, ensuring your emotional well-being remains nurtured and resilient.

Avoid the Mirror of Manipulation

Narcissists often excel at manipulation, using charm to draw others into their orbit. Be vigilant about their attempts to shift blame, guilt-trip, or distort reality. Maintain your sense of self and critical thinking, resisting the allure of their reflective tactics.

Mastering the Art of Empathetic Detachment

Imagine cultivating emotional armor that shields you from the emotional turmoil narcissists may try to evoke. Practice empathetic detachment—a state where you observe their behavior without becoming entangled. This practice helps you maintain your emotional balance.

Choosing When to Walk Away

Sometimes, the healthiest choice is to remove yourself from the presence of a toxic individual. Like transplanting a struggling plant to more fertile soil, walking away preserves your well-being and gives you space to grow.

Journaling Prompts: Chapter Three

Reflection on Emotions: *Which emotion(s) resonated with you the most when reading this chapter? Why?*

Behavioral Transformation: *Based on what you've learned from this chapter, what specific behaviors or habits do you feel inspired to change or adopt? How do you plan to implement these changes?*

I am who I am `and that is enough

CHAPTER FOUR

Unmasking Intimacy: Attachment Styles

Introduction: The Ties that Bind (or Repel!)

"We are biologically, cognitively, physically, and spiritually wired to love, to be loved, and to belong. When those needs are not met, we don't function as we were meant to." - Brené Brown

Ever wondered why some people can't bear the thought of being alone while others are happiest in their own company? Or why certain relationships feel like you're stuck in a chaotic dance, forever stepping on each other's toes? Ah, my friend, let's journey through the universe of attachment styles. Just like our favorite ice cream flavors or our innate dance moves (you know, the ones that emerge after that second glass of wine), our attachment styles define the rhythm of our relationships.

Our story starts in the 1930s with Harry Harlow's notorious experiments with baby rhesus monkeys. He aimed to see if the babies would prefer food or comfort when separated from their actual mothers. They invariably chose comfort. Though, let's take a pause and emphasize: these experiments, by today's standards, are downright unethical and cruel. But what they unveiled was the essential need for attachment and closeness, affirming that the survival instinct goes beyond just hunger—it craves connection and security.

Fast-forward to the 1950s, and along comes British psychologist John Bowlby. He further expanded on this need for attachment by observing children's reactions when separated from their primary caregivers. His observations and studies laid the foundation for what we now understand as attachment theory.

We, humans, are wired to be close to our caregivers. This closeness isn't just about love—it's a survival instinct. When the people we depend on during our formative years don't provide the necessary security, it can lead to non-secure attachment styles. This instinctual drive stems from our early ancestors, where staying close meant safety from predators or external threats.

Our attachment styles form remarkably early—from infancy up to about three years. The patterns established during these initial years act as the blueprint for our future relationships. Here's a quick rundown:

Secure: Comfortable with intimacy and independence. Almost 50% of the population identifies with this style.

Anxious-Preoccupied: Desperately seeking validation and fearing abandonment. Around 20% of individuals resonate with this.

Dismissive-Avoidant: Prefers independence, often pushing others away. This is seen in about 25% of people.

Fearful-Avoidant (Disorganized): A mix of anxious and avoidant behaviors, found in roughly 5% of the population.

While John Bowlby might have laid the foundational stones for the attachment theory, the building truly rose with contributions from many psychologists over the years. Mary Ainsworth, for instance, introduced the "Strange Situation" study in the 1970s. In this pivotal research, she observed children's reactions to being left alone, then reunited with their primary caregiver. From this, she was able to distinguish between different attachment styles more concretely, adding depth to Bowlby's initial concepts.

Our attachment style often tiptoes around our subconscious, influencing our relationships in more ways than one. When our attachment needs aren't met, our shadow self can emerge, reacting from a place of fear or old wounds. By recognizing our attachment style, we can address these underlying triggers, leading to healthier relationships and a more cohesive sense of self.

What's beautiful about humans? Our capacity to change. While our early experiences influence our attachment style, it's not written in stone. With introspection, awareness, and a pinch of courage, we can shift towards a more secure attachment, improving our relationships and internal harmony.

Imagine dancing with a partner. Both need to be in sync. Understanding your attachment style and that of your partner (or potential partner) can create a dance of love, respect, and mutual understanding, devoid of missteps and unintentional toe-stomping.

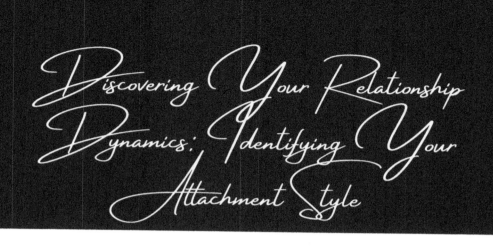

Discovering Your Relationship Dynamics: Identifying Your Attachment Style

"Our history is not our destiny." - Alan Cohen

The dynamics of our relationships often mirror our innermost feelings and fears. As we take this introspective journey, you might find yourself nodding, thinking, "Ah, so that's why I react this way in certain situations." Recognizing your attachment style can indeed offer those illuminating moments of self-awareness.

Secure Attachment

Statement 1: "I am comfortable getting close to others and trust that they feel the same towards me."

Statement 2: "When conflicts arise in my relationships, I believe they can be resolved through open conversation."

If you find resonance here, you may align with a secure attachment style, characterized by balanced relationships and effective communication.

Anxious-Preoccupied Attachment

Statement 1: "There are times when I worry about the depth of my partner's affection for me."

Statement 2: "I wish to be very close to my partner, but sometimes I fear it might overwhelm them."

Recognize yourself? You might lean towards the anxious-preoccupied style, often accompanied by a heightened emotional sensitivity.

Dismissive-Avoidant Attachment

Statement 1: "I value my independence highly and prefer not to rely on others."

Statement 2: "Deep emotional connections often seem more demanding than they're worth."

If these sentiments sound familiar, you could be oriented towards a dismissive-avoidant attachment, valuing self-sufficiency and personal space.

Fearful-Avoidant (or Disorganized) Attachment

Statement 1: "I have mixed feelings about close relationships. Sometimes I desire them, and at other times, I feel better keeping a distance."

Statement 2: "For me, trust can be a double-edged sword; it's essential, but also frightening."

If this strikes a chord, you might navigate the nuances of the fearful-avoidant style, often torn between intimacy and independence.

Remember, these are just initial insights into a more complex tapestry of your relational dynamics. As you evolve, so might your attachment style.

Reflect on past relationships. *Can you identify patterns that resonate with a specific attachment style?*

Think about your childhood. *How do you feel your early relationships with caregivers have influenced your attachment style?*

Imagine a relationship where you feel secure. What does it look like? How does it feel?

I am who I am and that is enough

CHAPTER FIVE

Mending the Broken Mirror: Trauma Healing

Introduction

"The wound is the place where the Light enters you."
— Rumi

Navigating the intricate maze of our personal wounds has brought us to this pivotal moment of reflection. Before delving further, it's essential to understand the trajectory of trauma healing, which largely falls into three defining stages.

Stage 1: Waking up to your Trauma - This is where most find themselves. A dawning realization, characterized by reading books, watching videos, or perhaps seeking therapeutic counsel. Yet, while there's abundant talking and thinking about the trauma, change remains elusive. The old patterns continue to resurface, playing out in a repetitive loop. It's not uncommon for many to linger here for years, often unknowingly.

Stage 2: Trauma Processing - The journey intensifies. Here, thinking gives way to doing. One starts delving deeper, confronting those haunting memories and emotions head-on. It's the emotional and somatic work that takes precedence. This stage is much like a rollercoaster — fleeting moments of triumph, followed by frustrating regressions. The teetering between past patterns and newfound awareness is palpable. Yet, with time and persistence, one begins to notice genuine shifts in behavior and personality.

Stage 3: Awakening - A stage where life is embraced in all its raw authenticity. Gone is the tumultuous rollercoaster, replaced by a profound resilience and equilibrium. There emerges a consistent confidence, a universal love, and a profound connectedness to all around us, heralding our deep communion with the universe.

As we transition from our recent discoveries, we're primed to journey further into the realm of healing and reconstruction. The broken mirror of our past, marked by fragmented and sometimes distorted reflections, beckons for restoration. Yet, this journey isn't merely about mending; it's about evolving. Our goal is to reshape this mirror into a beacon of clarity, strength, and wisdom.

Healing, in its essence, is both an art and a process. It beckons us to select the apt tools, foster the right mindset, and seize those defining moments of action. This chapter goes beyond sharing techniques. It's a heartfelt invitation to deeper self-awareness, illuminating not just who you were, but the boundless potential of who you can become.

So, with a mix of anticipation and curiosity, let's immerse ourselves in the practices that promise to guide our journey to healing.

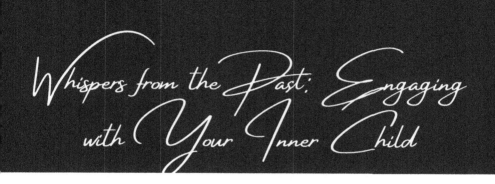

Whispers from the Past: Engaging with Your Inner Child

"It's never too late to have a happy childhood."
– Tom Robbins

Ever had that moment, sitting around the dinner table at a family gathering, and you and your sibling dive into a "Remember when..." story, but it feels like you're talking about two different planets? I mean, same living room floor for building Lego castles, same cartoons giving you Saturday morning life lessons, same parents giving you the "Because I said so!" speech. Yet, your memories? As different as apples and oranges!

Picture it this way: two artists, same sunset, yet one paints with warm oranges and reds, and the other captures hues of purples and blues. You and your sib? Both painting your childhood with your unique color palettes. Maybe your brother was the golden boy with the halo, while you sometimes felt like you had to pull off a magic trick just to be noticed. It's wild, right? How the same house can feel like a castle for one and maybe just a tiny bit like a dungeon for another. Every interaction, be it with parents, friends, or the kind stranger at the candy store, gets stored differently in our heart's memory vault. And in that vast sea of childhood memories, each little version of us holds a personal diary of emotions and tales.

Now, here comes the fun part. Ready to dial up your younger self? It's less "time machine" and more "heart machine," really.

Close your eyes. Think summer, age seven. Feel the sun on your skin. What are you wearing? Sneakers or sandals? Are you happy, or are those tiny brows furrowed? Dive into that. Or maybe another age is calling out to you? Twelve? Fifteen? That embarrassing day in high school? Go where your heart pulls. Trust me; it knows its way around.

Once you're there, imagine you're sharing a giant cookie and just... talk. "Hey, how was school today?" or "What made you so upset at that birthday party?" Open up the lines, and you'd be amazed at the stories that tumble out. And hey, journal this. I promise, the patterns that emerge? Gold.

Ever felt a weird flutter in your heart when someone forgot to call? Or that heavy lump in your throat when you entered a room full of strangers? These might just be the younger you tugging at your shirt, reminding you of moments they felt left behind or scared. These triggers? They're your roadmap. Dive in, explore, get curious. But remember, it's your journey. Your triggers, your landmarks. All unique.

But here's the kicker: Understanding is just the appetizer. The main course? Reparenting. Imagine if you could be the superhero for your younger self. Scoop them up, tell them they're seen, heard, and so very loved. This is your shot. Through conscious self-reparenting, you're not just patching up old boo-boos, you're belting out a lullaby for those old scars, letting them know it's okay to heal.

Missed that bedtime story? No worries! Become the storyteller. Craved for a comforting voice? Be that voice. Be the parent, the friend, the mentor you needed. Lay down that new track of love and understanding.

Embracing your inner child is like rekindling a deep, soulful relationship from the past. Each interaction is a blend of rediscovery, tender moments, and invaluable lessons. While the journey of reconnection can be lengthy, its rewards are profound and transformative. Consider this the very heart of trauma healing. Commit to this practice regularly, and watch as it becomes a guiding light on your path to healing and wholeness.

Journaling Prompts: Inner Child

Journey back to your childhood home. What feelings and sensations dominate? Describe the overarching mood of your household.

Reflect on your connection with your parents. What emotions and moments come to the forefront? Sum up the essence of your bond with them.

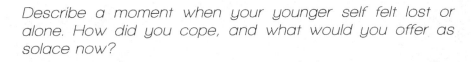

Describe a moment when your younger self felt lost or alone. How did you cope, and what would you offer as solace now?

Think of a time your younger self made a mistake and faced consequences. How did you feel then, and what would you tell your younger self now?

Write a comforting letter to your inner child. What do they need to hear from you today?

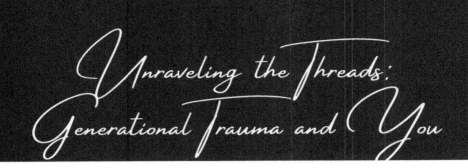

Unraveling the Threads: Generational Trauma and You

"Trauma in a family can resemble a relay race. Pain sprints from one generation to the next until someone breaks the cycle."
- Kristin Jones

Ever felt a strange, inexplicable fear, or found yourself facing issues that seem far bigger than your personal experiences would warrant? Well, there's a chance these aren't just your traumas. They could be the whispers of generations before you, passed down like old family recipes or heirloom jewelry. This is the realm of generational trauma.

Generational trauma, sometimes known as ancestral or intergenerational trauma, refers to the transfer of trauma from one generation to the next. If your grandparents or great-grandparents endured significant traumas, the emotional fallout of those experiences can echo through the family tree, touching branches far and wide.

Science is still delving deep into this, but emerging research suggests our genes can carry memories of traumas experienced by our ancestors. When events are that emotionally charged, they can leave a mark on our DNA, subtly influencing our behaviors, beliefs, and reactions.

Alright, time-traveler, now that we've dipped our toes into the pools of the past, how can we cleanse these waters for future generations? The first step is awareness. Recognizing that certain patterns or fears might not originate from our personal history can be liberating. It's like realizing you've been carrying a backpack filled with rocks that aren't even yours.

From there, shadow work becomes crucial. By diving deep into these ancestral patterns, we can start to heal not only ourselves but our lineage. It's like being the superhero your family lineage didn't know it needed.

A beautiful way to start is by charting your family history. Talk to elders, discover stories, and find patterns. Journal about them. This doesn't mean you'll solve the puzzle overnight, but each piece you lay down lights the path for both past and future generations. So, grab that lantern, and let's illuminate those generational shadows together.

Ancestral Echoes: *Are there any recurring stories or patterns you've noticed in your family history?*

Emotional Inventory: *List down any fears, reactions, or behaviors you have that don't seem to connect directly to your personal experiences. Could they be remnants of generational trauma?*

Treasured Tales: *Recall a story from your family's past that has been passed down through generations. How does this story make you feel? Can you spot any underlying themes of trauma or resilience?*

The Healing Hero: *If you were to imagine healing a specific trauma from your family's past, what would it look like? How would it change the narrative for future generations?*

Generational Gifts: *Trauma isn't the only thing passed down. Think of positive traits, talents, or strengths that seem to run in your family. How can these be used as tools for healing?*

Dialogue with the Past: *If you could have a heart-to-heart conversation with any ancestor, who would it be and what would you ask or say?*

Dreams for the Future: *Envision a future where you've played a role in healing your family's generational trauma. What does it look like for your children, grandchildren, or even great-grandchildren?*

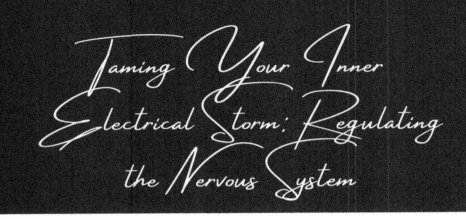

Taming Your Inner Electrical Storm: Regulating the Nervous System

"The nervous system holds the key to the body's incredible potential to heal itself." - Sir Jay Holder

Let's dive into the vast sea of our nervous system. Ever wondered why sometimes you feel supercharged and on other days you're more of a "sloth on a Monday morning" kind of vibe? Well, your nervous system plays a HUGE part in that. Think of it as the electrical system of your body — sometimes there's a surge and sometimes, well, a blackout.

Now, imagine if you had a dimmer switch for this system, where you could dial up your energy when you needed it and tone it down when you needed some calm. Intrigued? Stick with me, because this chapter's got the deets!

Before you can regulate anything, you need to know what's happening, right? Here's a quick breakdown:

Overcharged? Restlessness, racing heart, anxious thoughts, or feeling like you've had ten cups of coffee without the actual coffee.

Underpowered? Fatigue, feeling emotionally flat, lack of motivation, or like your batteries need recharging.

Let's Breath... Like we Really Mean It!

Breathing is like the universal remote of your nervous system. Deep, rhythmic breathing can calm the overcharged system, and energizing breaths can jump-start the underpowered ones. Try the "4-7-8" technique. Inhale for 4 seconds, hold for 7, and exhale for 8. Do it a few times and feel the magic!

Move that Booty!

Exercise isn't just for those abs and glutes. A good dance, a brisk walk, or even some stretching can help regulate your nervous system. It's like shaking off the excess energy or waking up your system.

Sleep: Your Nervous System's BFF

I can't stress this enough – get good sleep! It's like giving your nervous system a fluffy blanket and a warm cup of cocoa. It's the time it repairs, rejuvenates, and recharges.

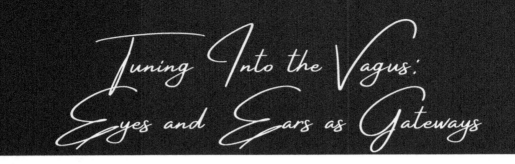

Tuning Into the Vagus: Eyes and Ears as Gateways

"When we activate the vagus nerve, we are tapping directly into our body's inbuilt mechanism for rest, repair, and tranquility."
— Dr. Navaz Habib

In the intricate web of our body's systems, the vagus nerve stands out as a particularly influential player. A bridge to relaxation and balance, the vagus nerve holds secrets that can help us bring calm to chaos. Interestingly, some simple exercises focusing on our eyes and ears can tap into this nerve's power, offering a much-needed respite.

In "Accessing the Healing Power of the Vagus Nerve," Stanley Rosenberg sheds light on the unique connection between our eyes and the vagus nerve. Here's how you can harness its power:

Position: Choose a quiet, comfortable place to sit or lie down, ensuring your head remains still and straight throughout the exercise.

Technique: Slowly turn your eyes to the far right, holding them there for 30 to 60 seconds as you breathe deeply. Gradually return them to center. Follow up by repeating the process to the left. This seemingly simple act of directing your gaze stimulates the vagus nerve, ushering in tranquility and equilibrium.

Our ears, often overlooked in relaxation practices, offer a direct route to calming our internal tempests. Here's how to engage with them:

Earlobe Massage

Using your thumb and forefinger, tenderly massage your earlobe in circular motions for 1-2 minutes, accompanying this action with deep, rhythmic breaths.

Ear Pull

Base Pull: Grasp your ear at the base, near where it attaches to your head. Gently pull your ear outwards and upwards, stretching it away from your head. Hold for about 15-20 seconds while taking deep breaths.

Side Pull: Next, grip your ear around its middle. Carefully pull it directly outwards, perpendicular to your head. Maintain this stretch for another 15-20 seconds, continuing your deep breaths.

Top Pull: Finally, hold the top portion of your ear. Gently stretch it upwards, as if you're trying to touch the sky with the tip of your ear. Retain this position for the last 15-20 seconds, syncing with your breaths.

By pulling the ear from various angles, you engage different facets of the vagus nerve, optimizing the calming and balancing effects of the exercise.

Behind-the-Ear Massage

Beginning at the earlobe's base, massage in an upward circular path, moving behind the ear, focusing especially on the bony region (mastoid bone). Dedicate 2-3 minutes to this, letting your breath flow deeply and calmly.

After completing the exercise, take a moment to relax and breathe deeply. Notice any changes in your body or state of mind. By engaging with such practices, not only do you complement your Shadow Work journey, but you also discover more about the marvelous mechanics of your own body.

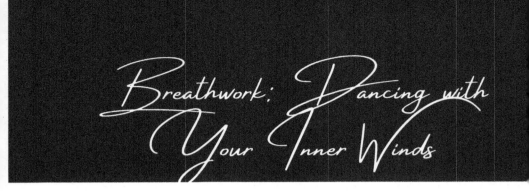

Breathwork: Dancing with Your Inner Winds

"Feel the energy of your inner body. Immediately mental noise slows down or ceases. Feel it in your hands, your feet, your abdomen, your chest. Feel the life that you are, the life that animates the body." – Eckhart Tolle

Alright, dear reader, pull up a chair (or a yoga mat). We're about to dive into one of the most profound yet often overlooked aspects of our existence: our breath. Imagine if every inhale could whisper secrets to your soul, and each exhale could sweep away the dust gathered from life's storms. That's the power of breathwork. And no, I'm not just talking about the same old inhale-exhale you've been doing since the day you were born. We're about to jazz it up!

Breathing 101: Not Just for Babies

I bet when you woke up today, you didn't think, "Hey, I'm going to learn how to breathe!" Yet, here we are! Most of us do "popcorn" breathing – quick, shallow, just enough to get by. But there's so much more to explore.

Fun Challenge: Lie down somewhere comfy. Place a book on your tummy. Your mission? Make that book rise and fall using only your breath. Feel the difference between chest and belly breathing. Do it till you feel like a breathing maestro!

Shake It Off: Breathwork for Emotional Spring Cleaning

Emotions. Those pesky little things! They sometimes sit heavy in our chest, like uninvited guests who overstay their welcome. Guess what? Breathwork is your polite way of showing them the door.

Quick Activity: Plant yourself in a quiet spot. Rapidly inhale three times through the nose, and then let out a looong exhale through the mouth, like you're blowing off steam (literally!). As you do this, picture releasing old, stagnant energy. Give me 5 minutes of this, and bask in the afterglow!

The Sacred Spaces In-Between

Life's not just about the ups (inhales) and downs (exhales). It's also about those magical moments in-between.

Mindful Minute: Tune into your breathing, focusing intently on the sweet little pause between inhaling and exhaling. It's like the universe's way of saying, "Hold on a sec. Relish this." It's a silent space but speaks volumes. Dive into its depths!

Building Bridges with Breath

Breath is the bridge between what's seen and unseen, known and mysterious.

Breathwork is like the secret sauce that adds zest to life. It's that magic potion that links us to the deepest parts of our soul, reminding us of our limitless potential. Each breath is an opportunity, an adventure, a story. So why not make it a best-seller? Dive in, dance with your breath, and watch the alchemy unfold.

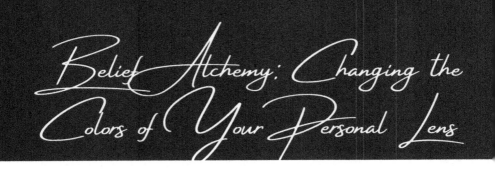

Belief Alchemy: Changing the Colors of Your Personal Lens

"Man is made by his belief. As he believes, so he is."
— Bhagavad Gita

Beliefs are a fascinating thing, aren't they? Think about it for a second. They're like those snazzy sunglasses you might wear on a bright summer day. At first, you're well aware of the tint – everything looks slightly blue or rose or even a deep shade of sunset orange. But after a while? You just might forget you're even wearing them, and the world's true colors? Oh, they get sneakily replaced by the hues of those glasses.

In a similar fashion, beliefs are thoughts we've wholeheartedly bought tickets to, convinced of their truth. They color our world, making us see life in unique, personalized shades.

Picture this: Amelia wakes up every morning, certain that the world is a treacherous obstacle course. She treads carefully, ever alert, seeing potential pitfalls in every corner. On the flip side, there's Alex, who wakes up with the giddy anticipation of a child at a candy store. He believes the world is a treasure trove waiting to be explored. Same dawn, same ambient sounds, same aroma of coffee – yet their day-to-day feels are vastly different, all thanks to their individual beliefs.

And where, you might wonder, do these silent scriptwriters of our lives come from? Most often, they're a legacy of our childhood, a product of our early environment. Remember that competitive cousin who always had to win at Monopoly? Or the ever-curious aunt who turned every dinner into a quiz night? Their influences, among others, were likely sowing the seeds of our beliefs.

Now, lean in for a quick brainy tidbit: every day, your mind juggles a whopping 60,000 thoughts! I know, right? It's like a non-stop chatter party up there. But the thing is, most of these thoughts are like dandelion seeds – they float by, and we barely notice. Only a select few dig their roots in, becoming our steadfast beliefs.

However, here's where it gets a tad tricky. Many of these beliefs prefer to work backstage, hanging out in our subconscious. This part of our mind isn't a fussy critic. It's more of an accepting sponge, soaking up whatever it's given without questioning the validity. So, if a thought like "I can't pull off those dance moves" or "I'll never nail that job interview" plays on repeat, the subconscious doesn't go, "Hold on a minute! Is that really true?" Nope. It just nods along, and soon enough, that thought hardens into belief.

To truly grasp the power of beliefs, let's jog back in time to 1954. A man named Roger Bannister did the impossible – he ran a mile in under 4 minutes. Before this, the world believed it couldn't be done. But once he smashed that barrier? It was as if he handed out invitations to the "Sub 4-minute Mile Club", and many athletes joined in. It wasn't some magical surge in physical ability that made it happen. Instead, it was a shift in belief about what was achievable.

So, dear reader, as we embark on this thrilling ride through the landscapes of beliefs, remember: while they might shape our view, they aren't set in stone. We can always change our glasses and, with them, the colors of our world. Strap in; this journey promises to be nothing short of transformative!

The Ego's Masquerade: Painting Over Old Portraits

"More the knowledge, lesser the ego. Lesser the knowledge, more the ego." — Albert Einstein

Ever strutted into a room feeling like you're wearing a mask? Not the decorative kind for a gala, but one that cloaks the raw, unfiltered you. Enter the realm of the ego—our internal master artist, sketching portraits with pastels from tales long gone.

Consider those labels we sometimes adorn ourselves with. "Oh, I'm naturally an introvert," or "Honestly, budgeting? Not my strong suit." But are these labels truly reflective, or just narratives we've spun, perhaps even borrowed from others? The ego excels in replaying past episodes, convincing us we're unchanged when in truth, we're living, evolving masterpieces.

While it's easy to view ourselves as mere products of our past, the real empowerment lies in recognizing our capacity to shape our futures. Dr. Joe Dispenza emphasizes that we can, through deliberate thought and intention, cast off the limiting beliefs our ego fiercely holds. He offers a metaphorical paintbrush, urging us to reimagine our life's canvas. Instead of old scripts, he beckons us to embrace fresh, vibrant narratives.

As we conclude our exploration of the ego, remember: it may try to cast us as static figures, but this is a fallacy. We are dynamic, constantly evolving beings, not explainable by stagnant beliefs.

Journaling Prompts: Identify a Limiting Belief

Reflect on a Challenge: *Describe a specific challenge or distressing situation in your life. How does it make you feel, and why is it significant to you?*

Emotional Core: *When you think about this challenge, what primary emotion surfaces? Is it fear, overwhelm, or perhaps another feeling? Elaborate on the emotion and its triggers.*

Seeking the Root: *Ask yourself, "Why does this situation evoke such a strong emotion?" Write down your answers, diving deeper with each response. Why does that matter? Why does it bother you?*

The Limiting Belief: *After your introspection, pinpoint the underlying belief that's contributing to your feelings about the challenge. What have you discovered about yourself and your perception of the situation?*

Understanding the Impact: *Reflect on your limiting belief. How has it shaped your emotions, self-confidence, overall life satisfaction, relationships, finances, and spiritual journey?*

Reflecting from Life's Twilight: *Imagine yourself at the end of your life, looking back. With this limiting belief having guided your journey, what do you see? Detail the potential losses, missed opportunities, and the emotional toll it took on your life's tapestry.*

Letting Go: *Write a personal commitment to release this limiting belief. Describe the physical sensations and feelings as you take a deep breath and let it out. What does letting go feel like?*

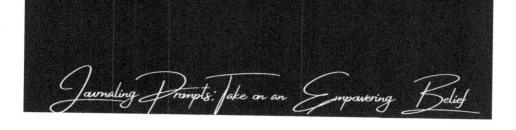

Crafting Empowerment: *Articulate a new, empowering belief to take the place of the old one. For context, if your limiting belief was "I always fail," your new belief might be "Every setback teaches me something valuable."*

The Power of Positive Thinking: *Dive deep into this new belief. Describe how adopting it could transform your emotions, boost your confidence, enhance your life satisfaction, improve your relationships, finances, and spiritual growth.*

Twilight's Silver Lining: *Project yourself to the end of your life, looking back. With this empowering belief as your guiding star, what legacy unfolds before you? Elaborate on the triumphs, cherished moments, and the depth of joy and fulfillment it brought to your life's narrative.*

Sealing the Deal: *After visualizing this positive future, reaffirm your commitment to this belief. Describe how it feels to fully embrace it, the physical sensations accompanying this acceptance, and any actions you'd like to take in celebration*

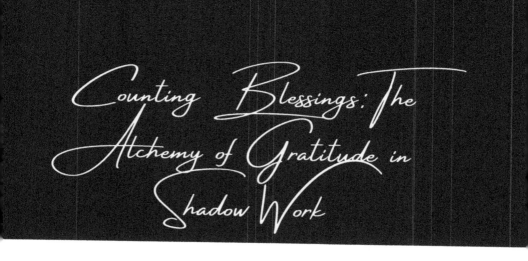

Counting Blessings: The Alchemy of Gratitude in Shadow Work

"Walk as if you are kissing the earth with your feet."
- Thich Nhat Hanh

The Not-So-Simple Joy of the Simple Things

Remember those childhood days when the world was one grand adventure? When a cardboard box was not just a box, but a spaceship, a castle, or a secret hideout? Somewhere along the winding path of adulthood, laden with bills and responsibilities, that wonder often dimmed. But the good news? We're here to spark it back up.

Gratitude Amidst the Storms

Life isn't just a string of rainbows; sometimes, it throws in a good old thunderstorm. But even amidst the tumultuous times, there exists a silver lining, a lesson to be tucked away, something—however minuscule—to be grateful for. And oh, the revelations! Perhaps a tough phase taught you resilience, or it showed you the kindness of a stranger, or maybe it simply revealed an inner strength you never knew you had.

The Fundamental Shift of Gratitude

Now, here's the kicker: gratitude isn't just a warm, fuzzy feeling; it fundamentally alters our state. You see, when we immerse ourselves in gratitude, our focus shifts. Instead of dwelling on what's missing or what went wrong, we start to notice the abundant goodness around us. This doesn't just change our mood—it rewires our brain. As we continually find things to be grateful for, our brain, being the adaptable organ it is, starts defaulting to positivity and resilience. In essence, gratitude acts as a neural massage, kneading away negativity and stress to make room for hope, joy, and optimism.

Building Your Gratitude Muscles

Just like a muscle, the more you flex your gratitude, the stronger it gets. The beauty of it? It's a transformative practice, altering not just your perspective but the very fabric of your experiences.

Passing the Gratitude Baton

Let's not forget, gratitude isn't merely a personal affair. It ripples outward. A genuine compliment here, a heartfelt thank you there—it sets off a chain reaction of kindness and appreciation.

Journaling Prompts: Gratitude

List down every little thing that made you smile or feel good in the past 24 hours. No joy is too minuscule!

Reflect on a challenging time in your life. With the wisdom of hindsight, what elements of gratitude can you unearth from it?

Spend a moment each day for a week noting down three things you're thankful for. How does this practice shift your mood or perspective as days go by?

Once a day, for a week, express your gratitude to someone. Note down their reactions and how it made you feel.

Mind Mastery: The Art of Selective Listening

"Don't believe everything you think. Thoughts are just that — thoughts." - Allan Lokos

Imagine sitting at a bustling café. The clink of coffee cups, chatter of countless conversations, the distant hum of traffic outside—it's a symphony of life unfolding in real-time. Now, out of all this noise, try focusing on just one voice or one sound. Difficult, isn't it? Similarly, our minds are ceaselessly chattering, throwing up thoughts, judgments, memories, and what-ifs at us like an overenthusiastic radio jockey. But here's a fun twist—you have the power to tune in (or out) as you wish!

Our minds are incredible tools, possessing the power to create masterpieces or weave webs of self-doubt. Throughout our lives, we've been conditioned to heed every thought, taking them as gospel truth. But, let's spill some tea—just because you have a thought doesn't mean it's an absolute fact.

Shadow Work teaches us to observe our thoughts, acknowledging their presence without getting lost in them. Picture it this way: thoughts are like clouds drifting across the sky of your awareness. Some are fluffy and light, others dark and stormy. But remember, beneath them lies the endless expanse of your true self—unchanging, ever serene.

Choosing which thoughts to engage with is a dance, a delicate balance between insight and instinct. Not every thought requires action. And not every worry deserves your worry. When you learn to listen with discernment, you're no longer at the mercy of every passing thought. Instead, you become its master, deciding when to engage and when to let it drift by.

So, how do you hone this selective hearing without coming off as someone ignoring the universe's calls?

Imagine your mind as a radio. What stations (thoughts) do you frequently tune into? Are they uplifting or draining?

Reflect on a recent thought that caused distress. Was it rooted in reality or a perceived reality? How did you respond?

Reflection on Resonance: *Which technique(s) felt just right or spoke to you most deeply? Why?*

Mapping the Journey: *How do you envision incorporating your chosen technique(s) into your daily or weekly rhythm?*

I am who I am and that is enough

CHAPTER SIX

How Dreams Illuminate the Self: Dream Analysis

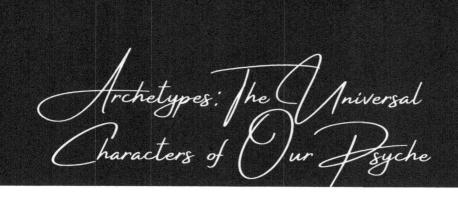

Archetypes: The Universal Characters of Our Psyche

"The archetype is a tendency to form such representations of a motif – representations that can vary a great deal in detail without losing their basic pattern." - Carl G. Jung

You know those stories that resonate with you, no matter where you're from? Like the fearless warrior, the nurturing mother, or that sneaky trickster that just makes you grin? Ever wondered why? Dive in with me as we uncover the timeless characters that play on the global stage of our minds.

Archetypes. It might have the ring of a word you'd hear in a dusty old library, but hold onto your hats, it's way more exciting than you think. At their core, archetypes are universally recognized symbols or characters that pop up in stories, myths, and even our dreams. Carl Jung, our main man in this journey, believed these characters reside in our collective unconscious, connecting all of us through shared human experience. It's like the universe gave us a communal toy box, and these archetypes are the favorite action figures we all play with!

Common Archetypes

You've probably bumped into these characters without even knowing it!

The Hero: Not always the guy with the cape. Sometimes it's that determined single mom or the student standing against bullying.

The Mother: Ever felt an overwhelming urge to care for something or someone? That's The Mother archetype, the embodiment of nurturing and protection.

The Shadow: Oh, you know this one! It's the dark twin, the Mr. Hyde to our Dr. Jekyll, representing the parts of us we often deny.

The Wise Old Man: That Gandalf-like figure who drops wisdom bombs when you least expect it.

And these are just the tip of the iceberg! From the stories of Hercules in Greece to Hanuman in India, different tales, but don't they feel kinda... the same? That's the magic of archetypes! They're like the seasoning in a dish, giving flavor to stories across cultures. While the plot changes, the essence - those archetypal themes - remain universally delicious!

Alright, real talk. While these archetypes are universal, they're also deeply personal. Remember that time you stood up for what you believed in? A little 'Hero' action there! Or when you comforted a friend in distress? That's 'The Mother' in you shining through. Our unique lives color these archetypes in special shades, making our connection to them as personal as our favorite song or our first love.

Ever had that déjà vu feeling watching a movie or reading a book? Like, "Hey, this feels familiar!" That's because archetypes don't just stay on pages or screens. They play out in our choices, the roles we assume, and even in those we admire or despise. Recognizing these patterns can be both fun and enlightening. It's like spotting Waldo in a crowd!

Embarking on the journey of understanding archetypes is like being handed a map to navigate the vast landscape of our minds. And as we move ahead, diving into the realm of dreams and self-reflection, having this map will make all the difference. So, buckle up, because knowing these archetypal buddies equips us to better interpret the grand drama of our lives. And oh boy, what a drama it is!

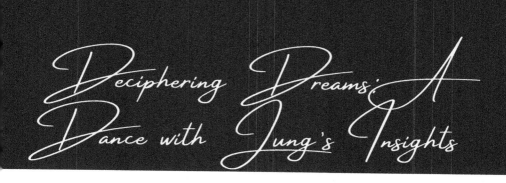

Deciphering Dreams: A Dance with Jung's Insights

"One does not dream; one is dreamed. We undergo the dream, we are the objects of the dream action, and not the actor." – Carl G. Jung

So, after a long day of introspection, you curl into your bed, hoping for a night of sweet dreams. But then, your mind has different plans. An endless staircase you can't quite reach the top of, a looming shadow you can't quite identify or showing up to an important event without any shoes? Yep, our dream world is indeed a curious realm. Now, what if I told you those weird, wonderful, or sometimes wacky dreams have a profound story to tell? We're about to waltz through the fascinating world of Carl Jung's dream analysis!

Dreams, according to Carl Jung, are our psyche's way of communicating. Think of them as nightly shows your mind puts on, especially for you! Every character, object, and bizarre scenario? They are all symbols loaded with meanings.

Tapping into Universal Symbols through the Collective Unconscious

Jung's belief in the collective unconscious—a reservoir of shared memories, symbols, and experiences that span across humanity—serves as the foundation for this. So, when your dreams present symbols, they may be drawing from this vast collective pool. That formidable dragon might be a universal symbol of challenge or fear. But, when it's donning your grandma's spectacles? That's when your individual psyche adds its own splash of color to the canvas!

The Compensation Theory

Ever felt like your dreams are contradicting your waking life? Welcome to Jung's compensation theory. He suggested that dreams often show us the opposite of our conscious attitudes. Let's say you're Ms. or Mr. Confidence during the day. But then you dream of standing on a stage, forgetting your lines. That's your unconscious hinting that maybe, just maybe, there's a speck of doubt or insecurity you need to address. It's all about balance.

Emotions in Dreams — The Unseen Narrators

The dream's plot might be wacky, but the emotions they evoke? Pure gold. Whether it's the anxiety of missing a flight or the elation of reuniting with a loved one, our feelings often hold the key to decoding the dream's message. It's not just about the what but the how it made you feel.

Reoccurring Dreams — The Persistent Callers

Ever had a dream that keeps repeating? It's like your subconscious is that friend who keeps calling until you pick up. It's desperate to tell you something! Whether it's facing a fear or resolving a past issue, these persistent dream sequences demand our attention.

Active Imagination — A Dialogue with the Dream

Jung introduced a nifty technique called 'Active Imagination.' It's a conscious dive into the dream while awake. Imagine revisiting the dream and interacting with its characters, asking them questions. It's like hopping back into a paused movie and changing its direction. A transformative tool for introspection, indeed!

Engaging with Dream Symbols

Ready to dive deep? Here's where the magic happens. The moment you wake up—yes, right then—grab that dream journal of yours. Why the urgency? Because dreams have a sneaky way of slipping through our fingers the longer we stay awake. The freshest details, the most vivid colors, the strangest twists—they're all most accessible immediately upon waking. So, scribble down everything: emotions, hues, objects, and yes, even the outlandishly bizarre bits.

Now, time to channel your inner detective. Dissect those symbols. Did you dream of a house? Ponder on what 'home' signifies to you. Is it a haven of safety? A reminder of family? A vault of hidden secrets? Maybe echoes of the past? Every symbol in your dream is like an onion, and your mission, should you choose to accept it, is to peel back the layers, one tear-jerking revelation at a time. Dive in, dreamer!

While Jung gave us the tools and theories, you are the best interpreter of your dreams. Trust your gut feelings. Sometimes a cigar might just be a cigar, or it could be a symbol of desire, power, or something entirely different. Dive deep, be curious, ask your inner self questions, and most importantly, enjoy the journey of self-discovery through the whimsical world of dreams!

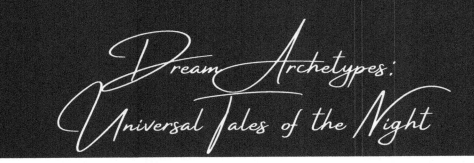

Dream Archetypes: Universal Tales of the Night

"In each of us there is another whom we do not know. He speaks to us in dreams and tells us how differently he sees us from the way we see ourselves." - Carl G. Jung

Ever been caught in a free fall during a dream? Or that classic "chased-by-something-terrifying" scenario? Maybe you've strutted confidently into a room only to discover you've forgotten your, well, everything? These aren't just random episodes; welcome to the world of dream archetypes.

In the vast cinema of our dreams, there are blockbusters shared from New York to Berlin, tales familiar from skyscrapers to ancient castles. Why? These dream archetypes are like the chart-toppers of the collective unconscious. Dive in, and let's spotlight some of these global favorites!

The Great Plunge: Ah, the age-old falling dream. More like a plummet into the abyss of anxiety or insecurities, right? While it can jolt us awake, it often hints at our inner fears of losing control or facing unexpected changes.

Run, Forest, Run!: Being chased in dreams is less about training for a marathon and more about confronting situations we're trying to dodge in our waking lives.

Soaring High: Unleash those wings! Flying represents our innermost desires to break free, touch the skies, or perhaps munch on some metaphorical freedom fries.

Lost in the Maze: Ever felt like you're stuck in a labyrinth or climbing an endless staircase? It's like your subconscious is telling you you're caught in a real-life loop or challenge.

Pop Quiz Nightmares: No, you didn't forget to study for that surprise test. It's your brain processing anxieties about performance, responsibility, or missing out on the latest season of your favorite show (kidding about the last one, or am I?).

Birthday Suit Bloopers: Ahem! Public nudity dreams might just be your psyche's cheeky way of dealing with feelings of exposure, vulnerability, or maybe just an overdue laundry day.

Mortality Musings: Death dreams are less about morbid fascinations and more symbolic of change, transformation, or that gut-wrenching season finale you watched last night.

Waves of Emotion: Water in its myriad forms (still, turbulent, cascading) mirrors our emotions, life stages, or that one time you forgot your umbrella.

Wild Kingdom: From protective lions to sneaky serpents, the animals of our dreams channel our raw instincts, desires, and, occasionally, that one embarrassing dance move.

But here's the catch: while these dream archetypes are universal, their interpretations are as unique as your coffee order (Extra foam? Almond milk? Two shots?). Your experiences, memories, and the latest drama with your neighbor's cat all add personal nuances to these shared stories.

So, next time you wake up puzzled by a dreamy escapade, remember: you're part of a global dream club, experiencing tales as old as time, yet tailor-made just for you. Sweet (or surreal) dreams!

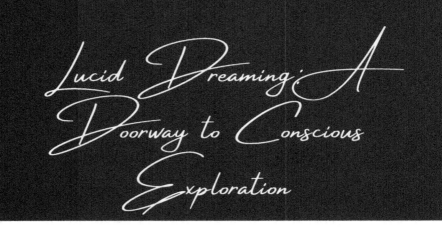

Lucid Dreaming: A Doorway to Conscious Exploration

"The dream is the small hidden door in the deepest and most intimate sanctum of the soul, which opens to that primeval cosmic night that was soul long before there was conscious ego and will be soul far beyond what a conscious ego could ever reach." - Carl G. Jung

Picture this: You're dreaming of wandering through a maze of cobblestone streets in a city reminiscent of Rome. But suddenly, a light bulb goes off. You realize, "Hey, I'm dreaming!" And just like that, you've entered the intriguing realm of lucid dreaming.

The Allure of Lucid Dreams

Lucid dreaming is the art and science of being aware that you're dreaming while you're in the dream. It's like unlocking a secret level in a video game, where suddenly the rules change and you have the cheat codes. Historically, cultures from Tibetan Buddhists to indigenous tribes in the Americas have recognized and harnessed the power of lucid dreaming for spiritual growth, problem-solving, and artistic inspiration.

Why Dive into Lucid Dreaming?

Beyond the undeniable cool factor, why should you care? Well, when you're lucid in a dream, you can actively engage with your subconscious. This is invaluable for shadow work. Imagine confronting a fear, asking it questions, or simply understanding its origin. Lucid dreaming can be a bridge to deeper introspection.

Tips for Becoming a Lucid Dreamer

Dream Journaling: Just like in our earlier discussion about dream analysis, maintaining a dream journal is vital. It not only helps you remember dreams but can also boost your awareness of being in a dream state.

Reality Checks: Throughout the day, ask yourself, "Am I dreaming?" It sounds silly, but if done consistently, you'll start asking the same question in your dreams. When the answer is "yes," boom, you're lucid!

Mnemonic Induction: Before sleeping, repeat to yourself, "I will know I'm dreaming." It's a simple affirmation, but it primes your brain to be alert during dream states.

Wake Back to Bed: Set an alarm for about 5 hours after you go to sleep. Wake up for a short while, then go back to bed. This method increases the chances of diving straight into a REM sleep stage, the prime time for lucid dreams.

Navigating the Lucid Landscape

Once you're aware within your dream, it can be overwhelming. Start slow. Try simple tasks like changing the color of an object or flying. With practice, you can delve deeper, maybe revisit those dream archetypes we discussed and interact with them.

Remember, the dream realm is malleable, shaped by thought and emotion. It's a playground for the psyche. As you gain proficiency in lucid dreaming, you'll not only have epic dream adventures but also glean deeper insights into your shadow self.

Lucid dreaming is a journey, not a destination. It's another layer in the beautiful tapestry of understanding oneself. Embrace it, explore it, and most importantly, have fun with it! After all, who wouldn't want to soar over the Grand Canyon or waltz with their shadow under the moonlight? Safe travels in your dreamscapes!

I am who I am and that is enough

CHAPTER SEVEN

Integrating Shadows, Unveiling Unity: The Spiritual Dimension of Shadow Work

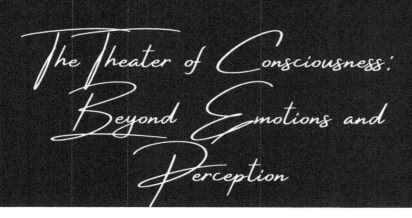

The Theater of Consciousness: Beyond Emotions and Perception

*"Reality is merely an illusion,
albeit a very persistent one."
– Albert Einstein*

Roll out the red carpet, grab your snazziest outfit, and perhaps a monocle if you're feeling extra, because we're taking a grand tour of the most extraordinary theater ever: your consciousness. Hold onto that popcorn because things are about to get enlightening!

Imagine standing in the midst of a bustling city square. Zooming cars, lively pedestrians, and yes, street performers flaunting their fiery juggling skills. Why? Because life is a delightful mix of the expected and unexpected. Now, every honk, every patter of rain, is akin to the myriad feelings stirring within us. But wait a minute! Though this buzzing scene might be chaotic and full of life, you are not in the thick of it. Instead, you're the cool observer from that balcony café, taking a sip from your favorite brew and watching life unfold.

This urban scene paints a vivid picture of our emotional world. Emotions, with all their drama and unpredictability, are like the elements of this city square. They appear, make their presence felt, and then move on, making way for the next experience.

Now, switching gears a tad, let's walk into that posh movie theater in your mind. The one where memories, dreams, and, okay, even that random thought about adopting another cat, play out like cinematic masterpieces. It's a space where every emotion, be it the thrill of adventure or the pang of nostalgia, gets its moment in the spotlight.

But – and this is the golden ticket – you aren't the fleeting scenes on that screen. You're the entire cinema hall! The ambiance, the plush seats, the dim lights setting the mood. Heck, you're even the buttery aroma wafting from freshly popped corn. What's playing out on the screen is but a minuscule part of who you truly are.

So, when that intense emotion, say a gust of anger or a whirlwind of excitement, knocks on your consciousness, picture it as a lively performer on your city square stage or a gripping scene on your inner movie screen. You can engage with it, appreciate its essence, or even chuckle at its quirks. But always remember, it's a transient guest, making a brief appearance in the vast auditorium of your being.

How about a quick escape to this theater?

Cosy Corner: Nestle into a snug spot. Blankets, cushions – go wild!

Silver Screen Magic: Eyes closed, envision your vast inner movie theater. Comfy seats, shimmering screen, and an ambiance of anticipation.

Now Showing: Observe the scenes unfolding. Memories, whimsical dreams, or maybe just that persistent thought about pineapple on pizza (it's a debate, I know).

You, the Majestic Cinema: As you tune into the movie, also sense the vast space around. The vastness that is so you. The theater that makes all the screenings possible.

Deep breath in. Slowly out. And, scene!

Understanding that we're more than just the actors in our emotional dramas, or even the stories we tell ourselves, is revolutionary. We are the vast backdrop against which all these tales unfold. Emotions, delightful and daunting, are but brief acts in our eternal play.

Embracing this perspective is akin to holding a master key to the world of Shadow Work. As we delve into its depths, we come armed with the wisdom that, even as we traverse through scenes of joy, sorrow, love, and beyond, we remain the timeless theater, honoring and cherishing every act with boundless love and grace.

Now, armed with this fresh perspective, let's journey further. Remember, in the grand story of life, you're both the writer and the audience. The play, no matter how riveting, is but a moment. You, my friend, are the eternal saga.

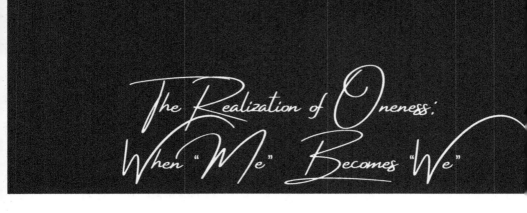

The Realization of Oneness: When "Me" Becomes "We"

"In the sky, there is no distinction of east and west; people create distinctions out of their own minds and then believe them to be true."
– Buddha

Do you remember the last time you stared up at a starlit sky, marveling at the vast expanse and feeling... strangely connected to it all? Well, buckle up, stargazer, because we're about to dive into one of the most profound and heart-warming truths of our existence. It's the realization that, despite all our perceived differences, we are all one.

Here's a fun tidbit: every atom in our body was once part of a star. Yep! We're all essentially cosmic stardust. Neat, huh? But let's zoom in a little. Not just the stars, but the trees, the birds, your neighbor's cat, the barista who always remembers your favorite brew – we're all intricately connected in the grand web of existence. It's like a cosmic dance, and each of us plays a vital role.

You know that feeling when someone ahead of you pays for your coffee in a drive-thru? It's unexpected, delightful, and guess what? You're more inclined to pass that kindness forward. That's the ripple effect. Now, imagine realizing that every action, thought, and emotion you experience impacts the whole. It's like throwing a pebble into a pond. The ripples spread out, touching everything in their path.

Understanding our interconnectedness means recognizing the power of our personal ripples. It shifts our perspective from "What's in it for me?" to "How can my actions benefit the whole?"

It's a common misconception that we're here on a quest to become "whole." But what if I told you that you're already whole, right now, just as you are? You see, if we're all connected, then each of us is a reflection of the entire universe. There's nothing to add, nothing to subtract. We're perfectly whole.

And this isn't just a comforting thought. Embracing this realization has transformative effects on relationships, emotions, and challenges. Imagine approaching conflicts or hurdles with the understanding that they're not just about "you versus them." Instead, they're opportunities for the collective "we" to learn and grow.

Fancy a cosmic connection? Let's take a brief journey together.

Setting the Stage: Find a peaceful spot to sit. Imagine you're about to plug into the universe. Exciting, right?

Breathing the Cosmos: Inhale deeply, imagining you're drawing in the energy of the stars, the oceans, and every living being. As you exhale, visualize sharing your unique essence with the universe.

Heartbeat of the World: Tune into your heartbeat. Now, imagine syncing it with the heartbeat of every person, animal, and plant. Feel the rhythm of collective existence.

Unity Visualization: Picture a golden thread connecting you to everything around. Feel the warmth, the bond, and the shared experience.

Closing the Loop: Taking a deep breath, and as you release, feel an immense gratitude for this shared journey we call life.

Dear soul explorer, realizing our oneness is like finding a treasure map where X marks every spot. The treasures are the moments of connection, shared laughter, mutual growth, and collective healing. As you continue your Shadow Work, remember that every shadow and every light you encounter is a part of the grand, beautiful whole.

And just like that starlit sky, we're all shining together, creating constellations of memories, experiences, and love. Here's to the magic of unity in our beautifully diverse cosmic dance!

Wholeness Over Achievement

"The privilege of a lifetime is to
become who you truly are."
- Carl G. Jung

Ahoy there, fellow traveler! Fresh off our grand adventure into the vast theater of our consciousness, we're going to set sail into another profound territory. Picture it: a world where you're already a dazzling gem, not needing any more polish or any validation. A world where the race for achievements takes a backseat, and the gentle embrace of our intrinsic wholeness steers the wheel.

In today's fast-paced world, where our worth is often measured by our achievements, accolades, and Instagram likes (oh, the tyranny of the double-tap!), it's ever so tempting to feel incomplete without these badges of honor. But let's pause and consider this: what if our inherent worth was like the vast, limitless sky, untouched by the fleeting clouds of external accomplishments?

Imagine you're at a magnificent orchestra. The musicians are in place, the audience is in rapt attention, and as the first note pierces the air, something magical happens. Every instrument, every note, every pause, contributes to the melody. Not one is more important than the other. The triangle's ting is as crucial as the violin's sweeping notes. This, dear reader, is the dance of wholeness. Each experience, emotion, thought, and shadow is a note in our life's symphony. None more pivotal than the other. They all play their part in the beautiful composition that is YOU.

From a young age, we're often sold the narrative that we're "almost there," but not quite. That there's always another mountain to climb, another goal to chase. But, my radiant friend, what if you already ARE the mountain, standing tall in your inherent majesty? What if the journey wasn't about reaching the peak, but realizing that the entire mountain, from base to summit, is you?

Your emotions, your dreams, your desires, even those pesky fears that pop up during a midnight snack run, they're all colors on your infinite palette. And guess what? Your canvas is already a masterpiece. You don't need to add more strokes to be complete; you just need to step back and appreciate the artistry that's been there all along.

As we delve deeper into our Shadow Work, it's crucial to remember that this isn't a project to "fix" or "complete" ourselves. It's about illumination. It's about recognizing that every shade, every hue of our being, contributes to our radiant tapestry. The shadows don't detract from our wholeness; they add depth and dimension.

So, let's make a pact. No more waiting for the next big thing to feel whole. No more holding our breath, thinking our next achievement will be the ticket to feeling complete. Because, darling reader, you're already there. You're the vast ocean, not just the waves. You're the entire enchanting forest, not just a tree. Celebrate your wholeness!

One Heart, One Universe: The Evolution of Boundless Love

"The only lasting beauty is the beauty of the heart." – Rumi

Alright, lovely reader! Let's take a moment and give ourselves a big, warm hug. Feel that? That's the embrace of self-love. But what if I told you that this same embrace can stretch, expand, and wrap around the entire universe? Oh, we're going on a journey that takes us from the cozy corners of our heart to the vast expanse of universal love. Fasten your seatbelts, or better yet, let's fly free!

Let's start within. Every time you show kindness to yourself, every time you forgive a past misstep, or pat yourself on the back for a job well done, you're nourishing your soul with love. It's like playing a gentle note on a piano that sends a beautiful echo throughout the room. This self-love isn't just a treat for yourself; it sends ripples across the universe.

Imagine building a house. Before you add the flashy windows or paint the walls your favorite shade of lavender, you lay a strong foundation. That's self-love. It's the base upon which the mansion of universal love is built. Without a deep, abiding love for oneself, how can one truly embrace the vastness of love that the universe offers?

When our hearts are full with self-love, a magical thing happens. The walls we've built, often unknowingly, start to crumble. We begin to see that the same spirit that dances within us twirls and swirls in every being. That annoying neighbor? He's dancing too. The barista who never gets your coffee right? Oh, she's part of the waltz as well. This realization is like opening a door to a room you never knew existed in your home, only to discover it's filled with treasures.

When we've bridged the gap between self-love and universal love, we've essentially stepped into an infinite ocean where every drop, every wave, every tide is a reflection of pure, unadulterated love. It's a space where judgments fade, where the boundaries between 'you' and 'me' blur, and where every soul is recognized as a shimmering star in a vast cosmic dance.

In the sphere of Shadow Work, as we uncover and heal, the practice of universal love plays a pivotal role. By embracing not only our shadows but the shadows of the collective, we foster a healing that's not just personal but planetary. As we hold space for our pain, our joy, our dreams, and fears, we learn to hold space for the world's.

Stepping into the realm of universal love is akin to realizing that the beautiful song in our heart is but a single note in the grand symphony of existence. And as our note harmonizes with the universe, the melody that arises is one of unity, compassion, and boundless love. As we wrap up this chapter, I invite you to take a deep breath, place a hand over your heart, and feel the pulse of universal love beating within.

I am who I am and that is enough

CHAPTER EIGHT

The Shadow Den: Your Sacred Journaling Environment

Anchored amidst Shadows: Staying Grounded

"To be rooted is perhaps the most important and least recognized need of the human soul."
– Simone Weil

The gentle tug beneath the surface... I bet you've felt it. It's like opening that old attic door, only to be hit with a gust of memories, some dusty, some sharp, all demanding to be seen. As we plunge into the depths of shadow work, sometimes we'll encounter pieces of ourselves that make us ask, "Is that really me?" But remember, these suppressed fragments were hidden away for a reason. Some were too painful, some too raw, and others just too darn inconvenient.

Let's face it; shadow work isn't a breezy stroll in the park. There might be times when you'll wish you could just flip a switch and illuminate all those shadowy corners instantly. But deep down, you also know that rushing might mean missing out on the very essence of the journey.

When the going gets tough, and those shadows seem a tad too dark or overwhelming, I want you to remember one thing: you have the tools to ground yourself. It's like having a trusty flashlight when you're navigating a dimly lit path.

So, why focus on grounding, especially during shadow work? Well, as you delve into those hidden parts, feelings like sadness, guilt, shame, or anger might surface. These emotions can send our nervous system into a little frenzy, akin to a rabbit sensing a fox nearby. When our nervous system is triggered, it's grounding techniques that can provide that security blanket, telling it, "Hey, it's okay. We got this."

Mindful Breathing: Your Trusty Companion in the Shadowlands

Setting the Scene: Begin by choosing a serene environment. It could be your favorite spot at home, a quiet corner in a park, or anywhere you feel safe and undisturbed. The key is to feel at ease.

Find Your Comfort Zone: Sit or lie down in a comfortable position. Use cushions or a blanket if you need. Remember, comfort is king here. If you're sitting, ensure your back is straight but relaxed.

The Breath Observer: Gently close your eyes. Now, without trying to change anything, notice your breath. Is it fast, slow, deep, or shallow? Feel the cool air entering your nostrils and the warm air leaving. This is about observing without judgment.

Deepen the Connection: Begin inhaling deeply through your nose. Imagine your lungs are like balloons, slowly and steadily expanding. Create space for the breath, visualizing it filling every nook and cranny of your body.

Belly Breathing: As you continue to breathe in, let your belly expand outward, not just your chest. It's a deep, nourishing kind of breathing. With each inhale, count to four, filling your belly like a gentle wave rolling onto the shore.

Extended Exhale: Now, as you breathe out, make it a tad longer than your inhale, counting to six or more if comfortable. Picture the wave receding, carrying away any stress or tension.

Rinse and Repeat: Continue this pattern for a few minutes or as long as you wish. With each cycle, feel yourself getting more anchored, more present, and more at peace.

The Rooting Visualization Exercise

Choosing Your Sacred Space: Begin by finding a serene spot, much like you did with mindful breathing. Maybe it's that comfy armchair, or beneath the tree in your backyard — somewhere you can relax and feel safe.

Getting Comfortable: Settle into a sitting or lying position. If you're seated, place your feet firmly on the ground, feeling the touch of the earth or floor beneath.

Closing the World Out: Gently close your eyes. Allow the external noises to fade. Imagine you're entering a sacred, internal space, a sanctuary of sorts.

Breathing Deeply: Start with a few deep breaths, inhaling through your nose and exhaling through your mouth. Feel the rhythm of your heartbeat, let it guide you.

Rooting Down: Now, visualize the soles of your feet. Picture them slowly growing roots, like those of an ancient tree. Feel them penetrating the earth beneath you, delving deeper and deeper. They navigate through layers of soil, rocks, and underground streams.

Embrace the Earth's Energy: As these roots travel, they begin to absorb the nourishing energy of the Earth. Feel this energy — it might be warm, cool, tingling, or simply comforting. This energy travels up through the roots, reaching your feet, legs, torso, until it envelops your entire being.

Feeling Anchored: As the energy fills you, feel the stability it brings. You're no longer a leaf being tossed around in a storm; you're the tree itself, standing tall, firm, and unwavering amidst any chaos.

Returning with Gratitude: When you feel completely rooted and present, gently retract the roots, visualizing them returning to your feet, leaving the nourishing energy within you. Take a few more deep breaths, expressing silent gratitude for this connection. When you're ready, slowly open your eyes, carrying this newfound strength with you.

There's an old saying, "You can't control the wind, but you can adjust the sails." In shadow work, when the winds of emotion get turbulent, this visualization can act as your anchor. Every time you feel adrift, unsteady, or overwhelmed, remember your roots. They're your silent, steadfast guardians, reminding you that no matter how stormy it gets up there, down below, you're firmly connected to the Earth, to life, to stability. So, dear explorer of the soul, remember this: the depths might be daunting, but with the right tools, there's no shadow too dark to illuminate.

Outer Sanctuary: Crafting Your Perfect Environment

"Your sacred space is where you can find yourself over and over again." – Joseph Campbell

Have you ever tried to cook in a messy kitchen? Pots scattered, spoons hidden, sauce spilling everywhere, and just when you're about to pour in that secret ingredient, the doorbell rings. Annoying, right? Now, think of your shadow work as a special recipe you're trying to master. To make it right, you need a space that's not just physically organized but energetically attuned. A space where your inner-chef can whip up miracles!

Picking Your Prime Time

Clock Watching or Intuition?: While it's tempting to squeeze in shadow work in those 'whenever' moments – right before bed, during a lunch break, or while waiting for your coffee to brew – there's a richer experience waiting for you when you choose wisely. Go for a time when you're feeling at your best – energetic, alert, and willing. This isn't about clock-watching but tuning into your body's natural rhythms. Are you a dawn person, feeling freshest with the morning dew? Or perhaps the tranquility of the night whispers secrets to you? Listen in!

Your Sacred Space

Nature's Embrace: Imagine journaling by a gurgling stream, the symphony of birds serenading you, as a gentle breeze rustles the pages. Nature, with its raw beauty and stillness, can be the perfect companion for shadow work. If you're fortunate enough to have a lovely outdoor space, or even a park nearby, let nature be your co-journalist.

Crafting Indoor Sanctuaries

Not all of us have the luxury of wandering into the woods whenever we feel like it. But here's the secret: you can bring nature indoors! Be it through potted plants, the sound of trickling water from a mini-fountain, or simply opening a window to let fresh air in. Create a space in your home where you feel cocooned, safe, and connected.

Tailoring Time and Routines

Duration Decisions: Diving deep into shadow work isn't a sprint; it's a marathon, sometimes even a leisurely stroll. Some days you'll want to journal for hours, and on others, just jotting down a few lines will feel enough. Start with allocating a set amount of time – say 20 minutes daily. As you progress, you can adjust this as per your intuition and comfort.

Consistency is Key: Remember that gym membership you took at the beginning of the year? We won't talk about how that turned out. But with shadow work, the principle remains: consistency breeds results. It's like watering a plant. Regular, nurturing attention helps it flourish. Decide on a routine, pencil it in your calendar, set a gentle reminder, and stick to it. Over time, this routine will become as natural as breathing.

In the end, this journey of self-discovery and transformation is uniquely yours. While guidance is great (and I'm here cheering you on every step of the way!), your intuition is your best guide. Mold your environment and routine to what sings to your soul. Remember, you're not just setting up a space, you're setting the stage for magic.

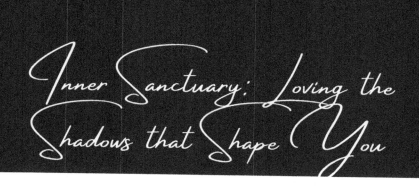

Inner Sanctuary: Loving the Shadows that Shape You

"Cut yourself some slack. You're doing better than you give yourself credit for. Self-forgiveness is a virtue." – Akiroq Brost

As we delve deeper into our personal terrains, remember that even in the murkiest of waters, there's a glint of clarity waiting to be found. Like that scene in old monster movies, the creature lurking in the shadows is often just misunderstood, seeking connection and love. Our shadows have their own tales to tell, and these tales, believe it or not, are stories of love in disguise.

Picture this: A dear friend comes to you, tears streaming down, confessing a mistake. Would you berate them, or would you open your arms, offering solace and understanding? Why should it be any different with yourself?

Often, we're our harshest critic. This self-punitive approach not only obstructs the path of shadow work but makes it thorny. By practicing self-forgiveness, we lubricate this journey, making it smoother and more meaningful. Every time you stumble upon a difficult revelation, whisper these words to yourself: "I forgive myself for not knowing better, for not doing better. I now know, and I will grow." This isn't just a mantra, but a magical elixir for your soul.

It was during one of my introspective dives that I stumbled upon a turbulent undercurrent of anger. At first, I was taken aback. Why was I harboring such rage, especially towards my parents, who I genuinely love? The realization wasn't immediate, nor was it comfortable.

Yet, as I sat with this anger, letting it envelop me rather than pushing it away, its message began to unfurl. It wasn't about resentment or rebellion. It was about me yearning to assert myself, seeking a space where my voice was acknowledged, my boundaries respected. This anger was a cry from a version of me that wanted to stand confidently in its truth.

In this revelation, I understood that my anger wasn't a destructive force but a protective one. It was my soul's way of urging me to honor my boundaries, to advocate for myself, to be seen and heard. It was, in essence, a manifestation of self-love.

Our Shadows, no matter how dark they might seem, are beacons guiding us towards our light. It's a journey, one where the road isn't always clear, but the destination, oh the destination, is a place of profound understanding and unwavering love.

Dealing with (Egoic) Resistance

"What you resist persists." - Carl G. Jung

You know those moments when you're on the verge of a breakthrough, and suddenly a voice chirps in, questioning, doubting, perhaps even mocking a little? Let's talk about that voice because it's not just some random inner critic—it's our ever-watchful ego.

Ah, the ego. It's like that older sibling who's overly protective, always on guard. When diving into the sometimes turbulent waters of shadow work, this vigilant part of you will inevitably sound the alarm bells. It might whisper, "Hey, are you sure you want to uncover that memory?" or more defensively, "This isn't going to help. Let's watch a movie instead."

But here's a fun twist: the ego isn't the villain in this story. It's the overcautious guardian, shaped by past battles, trying to shield you from more pain. It's seen the scars and wants to prevent new ones.

The key is not to battle your ego or shove it aside—because, let's be real, it's got some impressive resilience. Instead, try treating it like an old friend who sometimes worries a bit too much. Listen to its concerns, acknowledge them, and then gently, but firmly, let it know that you're choosing a different path this time.

As you continue your shadow work, it's crucial to recognize when the ego pops in, aiming to divert or protect. Thank it for its protective nature and then carry on with your journey, with the knowledge that healing requires venturing into territories the ego might find uncomfortable.

When Snails Fly: If You Want to Heal Fast, Go Slow

"Nature does not hurry, yet everything is accomplished." - Lao Tzu

Have you ever watched a snail on its journey? At first glance, it seems so incredibly... slow. But that snail, with its steady pace and unwavering commitment, gets to where it's going. Now, imagine if that snail had wings. Sounds absurd, right? But bear with me because, in the realm of shadow work, that's precisely what we're aiming for.

We live in an instant-gratification society. Want food? There's an app for that. Want to watch a movie? Click a button, and it's playing. But personal growth and healing? Well, there's no overnight express ticket for that journey.

And you know what? That's okay. In fact, it's more than okay—it's necessary. Imagine trying to rush through a beautiful scenic route, only catching blurred glimpses of the landscape. That's what hurried healing feels like.

Ironic as it may sound, taking your time can often lead to more profound, more lasting change. When you give each shadow its due time, you truly honor every part of you. You grant each suppressed emotion, each hidden memory, the respect of your full attention. And in doing so, you heal more deeply than if you had merely skimmed the surface.

So, how do we give our inner snails wings? By being intentional. By treating every session of shadow work not as a race but as a sacred ritual. Light that candle, brew that cup of tea, and nestle into your favorite nook. Breathe deeply. Dive into each emotion, each memory, no matter how painful, with love and compassion. And as you do, you'll find that your inner snail isn't just moving—it's soaring.

Cultivating a Relationship with Your Journal

"A journal isn't just a collection of writings, but a stage on which the self performs." - Irvin D. Yalom

Imagine, for a moment, being in a relationship with someone who never judges you, never interrupts, and is always there for you, day or night. Sounds ideal, doesn't it? Well, good news! You already have access to such a relationship: it's the one with your journal.

Your Journal, Your Confidant

When beginning Shadow Work, your journal becomes more than just a tool. It turns into a confidant, a therapist, a friend. It doesn't ridicule or scorn. Instead, it offers a safe space for you to untangle the threads of your thoughts, feelings, and experiences. Remember, it's not about writing for an audience; it's about writing for you.

Creating a Ritual

A relationship needs care, and like any other, your relationship with your journal flourishes with consistency. Create a ritual around your journaling time. Maybe light a candle, play soft music, or sip your favorite tea. This isn't just about writing—it's about immersing yourself in the experience.

Dates, Doodles, and Dreams

Feel free to personalize your journal entries. Date them, doodle in the margins, or stick in photographs or mementos. It's your space, and there are no rules. Over time, you'll find that these personal touches not only make journaling more enjoyable but also help you track your growth and transformation.

Having Conversations

It might sound a tad unconventional, but consider having a two-way conversation with your journal. Pose a question about a particular shadow you're grappling with and let your intuitive self-answer. This method can often lead to profound insights and resolutions.

Embrace the Evolving Relationship

Your relationship with your journal will evolve, and that's okay! There might be days when you pour pages of raw emotions, and others where you jot down a line or two. Some days, you might skip journaling altogether. Whatever the flow, honor it. Trust in the journey.

Remembering Your Why

When in doubt or feeling uninspired, remind yourself why you began this journaling journey. Your 'why' is the compass that'll steer you back to the pages, to introspection, and to healing.

In closing, your journal is more than just paper and ink. It's a tapestry of your soul's journey, woven with love, challenges, growth, and triumphs. So, treat it with kindness and reverence, for it holds the stories of your deepest dives and greatest ascents. Through thick and thin, in shadows and light, your journal stands by your side, ever patient, ever ready to embrace all that you are.

Know When to Expand Your Support System

"Individually, we are one drop.
Together, we are an ocean."
- Ryunosuke Satoro

Knowing when to seek external support is crucial. Are you feeling persistently overwhelmed or disconnected from your journaling process? Do certain shadows provoke disproportionate distress? These might be indicators that it's time to expand your circle of support.

Expanding your support doesn't mean an automatic visit to a therapist, though that's a valuable option. It could be joining a shadow work group, attending a workshop, or simply reaching out to a close friend or family member for a heart-to-heart.

If you do choose to engage with a therapist or counselor, remember, it's like forming any other relationship. It's essential to find someone you resonate with, someone who understands and respects your journey.

Consider the power of group dynamics. Group therapy or shadow work circles offer a space where stories are shared, and experiences mirrored. The collective energy of a group, bound by a shared intent, can amplify healing.

While it's imperative to know when to expand your support system, it's equally vital to recognize the balance. The interplay between solo introspection and external support can be magical. It's not an "either-or" but a harmonious "and."

Sacred Space Design: *Picture your ideal journaling space. What elements do you envision that can foster creativity and tranquility? What does it look, sound, and feel like?*

Finding the right Time: *Reflect on the rhythms of your day. When do you feel most introspective? How often would you like to dedicate time to shadow journaling? Is it daily, every other day, or weekly? Set realistic goals that honor your emotional bandwidth.*

Beyond the Pages: *Think of your journal as a living entity. How will you nurture this relationship? Perhaps you might want to set aside time every month to review and reflect upon your entries.*

PART II

Shadow Work

Journaling Prompts

CHILDHOOD

EARLIEST MEMORY

Describe your earliest childhood memory.
What emotions are attached to it?

CHERISHED TOY

Think of a toy or object you cherished as a child. Why was it special? How did it make you feel?

PARENTAL INFLUENCE

How did your relationship with your parents shape your early years? Were you closer to one parent?

CHILDHOOD FRIENDSHIP

How did you perceive the concept of 'friendship'
as a child? Who was your closest friend and
what made your bond strong?

LONELY MOMENTS

Think of moments when you felt misunderstood or alone as a child. How did you navigate those feelings?

INNER CHILD

INNER CHILD

Close your eyes and visualize your inner child. How do they look? What are they wearing? How do they feel?

INNER VOICE

If your inner child could speak to you right now, what would they say?

PAST HURTS

Think of a moment when your inner child felt neglected or hurt. How can you comfort and heal that pain now?

LETTER OF ASSURANCE

Write a letter to your inner child, expressing all the things you wish they had known growing up.

ACTIVE PRESENCE

In what situations does your inner child feel
most active or present in your adult life?

VALIDATING FEELINGS

How can you ensure your inner child feels seen, heard, and validated regularly?

RELATIONSHIPS

FIRST BONDS

Recall your earliest relationship, be it a friendship or romantic. What did you learn from it?

GROWTH TOGETHER

Describe a time when a relationship
helped you grow personally. What changes
did it inspire?

RELATIONSHIP PATTERNS

Have you noticed any recurring patterns or behaviors in your relationships? What might be the root cause?

BOUNDARIES

How do you establish and maintain boundaries?
Are there times you've compromised them,
and why?

SELF IN RELATIONSHIPS

How do you ensure you maintain your
individuality and don't lose yourself
in a relationship?

IDENTITY

CORE BELIEFS

List the beliefs and values that define you.
How have they evolved over time?

ROLE MODELS

Who are the individuals you've looked up to throughout your life? How have they shaped your perception of self?

EVOLUTION

How has your identity evolved from
your teenage years to now?

DREAMS

NIGHT VISIONS

Describe a recent dream you had.
What emotions did it evoke?

RECURRING SCENES

Do you have a recurring dream?
What themes or elements are consistent?

INTERPRETATIONS

Choose a dream you remember vividly.
How might you interpret its symbols or events?

FEARS

FEAR ORIGIN

Reflect on a fear you have.
When did you first become aware of it?

FUTURE FEARS

What are you most afraid of regarding the future?

OVERCOMING FEAR

Write about a fear you hope to overcome.
What steps can you take to address it?

SHAME WOUND

SHAME ORIGINS

What's the earliest memory
you have of feeling shame?

TRIGGERS

What situations or comments tend to trigger feelings of shame in you currently?

DEFENSES

How do you typically react or cope
when you feel shame?

BELIEFS

What core beliefs about yourself
does this shame highlight?

HEALING

Recall a moment when you overcame feelings of shame. What helped you in that situation?

TRUST WOUND

TRUST PATTERNS

Are there recurring situations or types of people that trigger your trust issues?

WORTHINESS

Are there underlying beliefs about not being
worthy of trust or loyalty from others?

SAFETY NETS

What conditions or assurances do you need to
trust someone or something?

ANGER WOUND

FIRST SPARK

Recall the earliest memory where you felt
intense anger. What were the circumstances?

TRIGGERS

Identify the common situations or
individuals that ignite your anger.

EXPRESSION

How do you typically express your anger?
Through words, actions, or internalization?

NEW NARRATIVE

Envision a situation that typically makes you angry. How can you reframe or respond to it differently?

AVOIDANCE
WOUND

AVOIDANCE ORIGINS

Trace back to an early memory where you first felt the urge to avoid something. What were the surrounding circumstances?

PROTECTION MODE

What do you believe you're protecting
yourself from by avoiding certain
situations or people?

EMOTIONAL IMPACT

How has consistent avoidance affected your emotional well-being and self-worth?

GROWTH ZONE

Think of a situation you've been avoiding.
How might confronting it lead to personal growth?

PARENT WOUND

ROLE MODELS

How have your parents' behaviors influenced
your own, both positively and negatively?

PARENTAL LOVE

How did each parent express love?
Was it in a manner you understood or craved?

ATTRACTION

How do the traits or behaviors of the partners you've attracted mirror those of your parents, both positively and negatively?

IDEAL PARTNER

Who embodies the qualities of your ideal partner?
What deep-seated beliefs might be preventing
you from attracting this individual in your life?

LIFE'S BLUEPRINT

DREAMS

If your life was a house, what rooms would it have? (E.g., a 'room' for family, career, passion projects, spiritual growth, etc.)

THE BOOK OF YOU

If your life was a book, what would the current chapter be titled, and what would you like the next chapter to be about?

DESIRED REALITY

Visualize the most genuine and fulfilling
version of your life. What stands out?

MANIFESTATION ROADMAP

How can you bridge the gap between your current reality and the life you'd like to see? List actionable steps to move closer to your envisioned future.

INNERMOST WISH

What is your innermost wish for this lifetime?

I am who I am and that is enough

BOOKS BY
FELIX R. BUCHWALD

A HEARTFELT THANKS TO YOU!

Through shadow work, you heal not just yourself but also ripple healing to your family, community, and the world beyond.

Writing this book (it's my first!) has been a transformative experience for me. I genuinely hope it brings you both joy and insight.

As a new self-published author, your support means everything. Whether you leave a review on Amazon, share a glimpse of the book on social media, or choose to do both, it would make a world of difference. Thank you for being part of my journey!

To express my gratitude to those who showcase the book on TikTok, Instagram, or Facebook, I offer a free advance ebook copy of my next exploration into Shadow Work. Just email your shared content to felix@felixbuchwald.com, and you'll be among the first to receive it when it's ready :)

QR Link to Amazon Review Page

Made in the USA
Las Vegas, NV
25 January 2024

84899376R00134